PRACTICAL ZEN

MEDITATION AND BEYOND

Julian Daizan Skinner

Foreword by Shinzan Miyamae

**SINGING
DRAGON**

LONDON AND PHILADELPHIA

Caution: The practices and techniques described herein are not to be used as an alternative to professional medical treatment. This presentation does not attempt to give any medical diagnosis, treatment, prescription or suggestion for medication in relation to any human disease or physical condition.

This material is intended to supplement individual instruction by a competent teacher. Anyone who undertakes these practices on the basis of this material alone, does so entirely at his or her own risk.

Zenways is not and cannot be held responsible for the consequences of any practice or misuse of the information presented here. Consult with your doctor before embarking on any meditation or exercise programme.

First published in 2017
by Singing Dragon
an imprint of Jessica Kingsley Publishers
73 Collier Street
London N1 9BE, UK
and
400 Market Street, Suite 400
Philadelphia, PA 19106, USA

www.singingdragon.com

Library of Congress Cataloging in Publication Data
A CIP catalog record for this book is available from the Library of Congress

British Library Cataloguing in Publication Data
A CIP catalogue record for this book is available from the British Library

ISBN 978 1 84819 363 5
eISBN 978 0 85701 321 7

Printed and bound by CPI Group (UK) Ltd, Croydon CR0 4YY

is a true beacon on the journ... ... all those
who wish to take it.'

> – Dr Russell Razzaque, founder of The College of
> Mindful Clinicians, author of Breaking Down is
> Waking Up and Obama Karma

'To those who find Zen somewhat intimidating, Daizan's relaxed
approach should be appealing; *Practical Zen* offers something
for everyone with an interest in Zen, with a plethora of ideas,
possibilities and suggestions for practice.'

> – Stephen Addiss, author of
> The Art of Zen and Zen Sourcebook

'The explanations and instructions are beautifully clear and the
structure really supports the transmission of these invaluable
practices. I particularly loved the sections on duality and
non-duality, the unborn, the hara, the ox and all the stories,
particularly the moving events around the temple fire. I
wholeheartedly recommend *Practical Zen*.'

> – Livi Michael, multi-award-winning novelist

of related interest

The Key to the Qigong Meditation State
Rujing and Still Qigong
Tianjun Liu
Foreword by Master Zhongxian Wu
ISBN 978 1 84819 232 4
eISBN 978 0 85701 177 0

Daoist Meditation
The Purification of the Heart Method of Meditation and Discourse
on Sitting and Forgetting (Zuò Wàng Lùn) by Si Ma Cheng Zhen
Translated and with a commentary by Wu Jyh Cherng
ISBN 978 1 84819 211 9
eISBN 978 0 85701 161 9

Tranquil Sitting
A Taoist Journal on Meditation and Chinese Medical Qigong
Yin Shi Zi translated by Shifu Hwang and Cheney Crow
ISBN 978 1 84819 112 9
eISBN 978 0 85701 090 2

CONTENTS

PART II: THE REST OF YOUR LIFE

FOREWORD

It is a pleasure for me to know that these practical methods of finding happiness and meaning, strength and power can at last be known and applied in the Western world.

Many Zen scholars have appeared; far fewer people have thrown themselves into the way of true training, forging a new body and mind. The writer of this book, my successor, Julian Daizan Skinner, has done just that.

He has guided many to the successful application of these ways of practice. Each year he brings Western students to Gyokuryuji Temple who are earnestly seeking awakening. I have seen with my own eyes that many find what they seek. This has been a great inspiration to Japanese students of Zen.

In this time of planetary ecological crisis, the world urgently needs true men and women whose life basis is deeper than mere materialism. May this book guide you to the practical achievement of the promise of Zen. May your practice benefit yourself, your family and the whole world.

Shinzan Miyamae, Gyokuryuji

ACKNOWLEDGEMENTS

This book could not have come into being without the guidance and blessings of my teachers over two-and-a-half decades, most particularly my primary teachers, Shinzan Miyamae Rōshi and Rev. Master Daishin Morgan. In addition, I am particularly grateful to Rev. Master Jisho Perry, who showed me what love means in a Zen context; Rev. Master Koten Benson, who repeatedly encouraged me to take the next step with trust in myself and taught me to pull forth the essence of the teachings from their cultural framework; Rev. Master Saido Kennaway, who taught me to look beneath the surface of situations and relationships while I served as his attendant for a number of years; Rev. Master Daizui MacPhillamy, who drew important links between Zen and Western psychology; Gensho Hozumi Rōshi, who generously shared his teachings on body-work and energy development; Nagasaki Shokyo Sensei, abbot of Kongofukuji, who opened up the area of managing energy in a new context; Okuda Donin Sensei, who showed me how a Zen monk can also be a very fine Shamanic mountain practitioner; Tada Katsuji Sensei, who allowed me to teach yoga in his temple, Saishoji; and Kuze Enju Sensei, who shared with me the living tradition of Enku's teaching.

I would also like to thank all the other teachers from whom I have learned over the years, particularly Father Jack Madden, who first taught me to meditate; Father Conrad Pepler OP, who explicated 'The Cloud of Unknowing', and drew links to Zen; Jhampa Shaneman and Lobsang Tulku, who taught me about the Tibetan tradition of inner fire; the unknown swordsman, who taught me the 'ah-un' breathing practice; Toshi Sato, who taught me the version of *naikan* described in this book; Aikido master Shuji Ozeki Sensei, who taught me how to relate energetics and physicality, as well as how to cook; Hideko Ikawa Sensei, embodiment of tea, who introduced me to the Urasenke school of tea ceremony; Nakane Masanori Sensei, who taught me *shakuhachi*, Zen flute; Mori Tomoko Sensei, who showed me what dedication to teaching yoga can look like; and Lawrence Noyes, who meticulously passed on the teachings of Charles Berner.

I want to express special thanks to my parents and family, who have provided a platform of generous love and support over the years of my search, and who did their best to understand my journey, and trusted me to find my own way. My father, Kevin, passed on his love of asking difficult and challenging questions and not settling for easy answers, and my mother, Judith, gave me her grounded and practical advice along the way, and was utterly unfaltering in her love. I would also like to acknowledge my sister, Annie Owen, who has been a soul sister as well as a blood sister, and edited the first ten or so drafts of this book.

I give special thanks to Stuart Horwitz, who picked things up where Annie left off; Samantha Warrington, who spent weeks helping to shape and clean up the manuscript; Mark Kuren Westmoquette, managing editor and conductor of the orchestra; Alex Horikitusne Reinke, artist; and Meijia Ling, Matt Shinkai Kane, Akane Moindron and Noriko Yamasaki, fellow translators. Thank you also to the Zen practitioners who graciously agreed to share their experiences for the benefit of others.

I especially wish to thank my friends, who have spanned continents and in many cases endured over almost two decades of separation. They have given me support of inestimable value. Sometimes just knowing that they were out there somewhere has helped, and at other times they have been nearby sharing their thoughts and insights: Rod Wooden (who got me going on the Zen road), Richard Penson, Francis Lobo, Charles Williams, Richard Dias, Carolyn Cassady, Justine Glenton, Brad Chia, Chris Uemura, Charlotte Esme Turner, Miho and Simon Werner, Bob Griffiths, Miho Ishihara, Sumiko Hayashi, Sue Skinner, John Boulderstone, Minke de Vos, Geoff Hornby and Paul Gent.

Since I've come back from Japan I've been particularly helped by Alistair Cunningham and Twobirds, Sir Richard Glyn, Mark and Becky Weber, Sabine Petukat, Dr Russell Razzaque from the College of Mindful Clinicians, who has been applying this work in the field of mental health, Barbara Ryusen Gabrys and Dr Maryanne Martin of the University of Oxford, Chris Owen, Jonathan Harrison, who found this book a home, Desmond Biddulph, Darcy Flynn and Ludmila Clement-Horton.

Over the bumbling course of this spiritual and physical journey, time and again doors have opened where they shouldn't even exist. I would like to extend my humble thanks and respects to the visible and invisible supporters, Buddhas and Bodhisattvas who made my travels possible, brought me the right people and the right information at the right time, and provided me with energy and perseverance while this book was being born. May they continue to guide this work toward those whom it will benefit! May any mistakes or omissions be forgiven, and may all beings be well and happy, awake and free.

INTRODUCTION

It was the beginning of April, the time when most Zen temples in Japan have an elaborate ceremony to mark the anniversary of the Buddha's birth. Instead, our Zen master, Shinzan Rōshi, had us out in the bamboo grove below Gyokuryuji Temple digging up fresh bamboo shoots to eat. The ease and vigour of his movements belied his 70-odd years. Bamboo roots are tough and awkward to dig, so after a few hours' work we rested in the shade drinking *mugi cha*, chilled barley tea.

Shinzan Rōshi sat beside me. 'No ceremony today,' he said. 'We make new baby Buddha like this.' He made digging movements with his hands.

I was new in the temple, having spent 14 years practising in a formal and tradition-minded Zen monastery in the UK. Shinzan Rōshi's freewheeling style and palpable joy was very different.

'Baby is very beautiful,' he continued. 'Human baby is just completely perfect. When hungry, it cries. When sleepy, it sleeps.' He smiled and added, 'Perhaps in Christian Bible, the Garden of Eden is like this baby time. But it is a very, very short time. We grow, study, leave the happy garden and long, long time, maybe longest of any animal, we grow. As we grow, grow, grow, the me, me, me is stronger and stronger. This is me.' He pointed to himself. 'That is world.' He pointed away.

'Adult time is split. Little me, great big world. This is needed. Adult person is responsible, so I must know myself, take charge of my life. I wanted to be big businessman, make money, build something.' He laughed. I had heard previously that his business ventures had been spectacular disasters.

'But also adult time is very lonely. Little me, great big world. That is why we practise.' He stood up. 'Our practice is to now dig bamboo.'

Over the following months and years, Shinzan Rōshi would frequently expand on these simple truths. Adulthood, the stage at which a person takes responsibility, is inevitably and inexorably the place of separation, a state that the existentialists liked to call alienation.

We come up with all sorts of strategies to manage this conflict and loneliness, investing in relationships, creativity, success, family life. But even the greatest successes in these areas can do no more than distract us from the fundamental split: 'Little me versus the great big world.'

Most adults, Shinzan Rōshi would claim, stop growing and stay in this state, this awful worldview. Life inevitably becomes a tragedy.

But fortunately there is more. The split worldview is not wrong or untrue; it is just partial. The oneness with the universe that we experienced in our infanthood is still available to us. This is by no means a regression; it is essential we remain adult and fully responsible, but we can nevertheless fully reconnect. We can come home in a way that encompasses both unity and duality, and this is the enlightenment of Zen.

Many people have experiences of wonder or joy, perhaps at times of falling in love or the birth of a child. But more fundamental and transformative than any experience is the shift in which all experiences can be seen with new eyes.

Nothing is changed, life continues, but we now find there is nothing to resist or defend against. We can be happy. We can know that on one level we are actually indestructible. Many of the Zen meditation practices in this book are designed to help you find this way.

More than this, the ancestors of the Rinzai tradition of Zen taught how to live a grounded, strong, energetic life, so you can make a difference in the world and be of use to others. This book also gives you very specific traditional practices to achieve this.

The process that led up to this book started when I returned to the UK in the summer of 2007. Shinzan Rōshi had named me as his successor and urged me to share what I'd discovered. I was broke, exhausted and without any connections.

I decided to walk. On Midsummer morning, 21 June, I set off from St Catherine's Lighthouse at the southern tip of the Isle of Wight and headed northwards. My projected route was straight up the middle of the island of Britain, 777 miles, according to Google Maps. The finish point was another lighthouse out on the high cliffs of Cape Wrath at the northern tip of Scotland.

I was wearing my Japanese monk's robes and a kasa, a broad-brimmed woven hat. I carried no money and resolved to keep things that way. I had my alms bowl and was hoping, somehow, to find food through people's generosity. I didn't really know how. The way we did it in Japan, standing in doorways with head down in a formal bow, face concealed and chanting a greeting, would never work in the UK. I was pretty nervous at the prospect of the pilgrimage ahead.

The sun was shining over the fields and quiet lanes. A few miles along the road a car pulled up beside me. A middle-aged woman wound down her window. I think she was called Sally.

'Are you Daizan Rōshi?' she asked. 'Will you teach me to meditate?'

Isle of Wight Radio had run a little story about an English Zen master who used to be a scientist in the pharmaceutical industry, now just back from Japan, and walking across the island on the way to Scotland. The woman was intrigued, so, once she'd dropped her daughter off at school, she drove around looking for me. She pulled her car into the grass verge. She sat on my rucksack. I showed her how to get started and we meditated together. The transplanting process had begun.

Since that time I've shared the methods of Zen meditation with thousands of people.

Over the intervening eight years, I've found that the particular practices originating in the Rinzai school and taught to me by Shinzan Rōshi are uniquely suitable for helping busy, stressed-out Westerners to find a source of sustenance and meaning in their lives, while at the same time building physical and emotional strength and energy. My own experience had led me to believe that this was the case. Sharing the work with others reinforced my conviction.

It takes a little time to learn and apply this material, but the effort pays off handsomely. I found there was too much for students to learn in a single session, so, once the walk ended up on Cape Wrath, I went to London and established an eight-week programme. Students could then really integrate each piece of the puzzle before exploring the next. In fact, I established two eight-week programmes. One is for people who want to use meditation to improve their lives simply on the health and wellbeing level. For the last thousand years or so, this type of practice has been called *bompu Zen* – literally, mundane or worldly meditation. The second course, the one contained in this book, is for people who want to look deeper, to find a whole new basis to life.

I've trained a group of instructors – about 50 at the last count – located in the UK, Europe, the USA and Japan – to teach this work person-to-person, and I think that's the best way to learn it. We have a 'find a teacher' page on our Zenways website (www.zenways.org). However, not everyone has the time or lifestyle to get to the same teacher for a couple of hours a week over eight weeks. For these people, this book offers a substitute. It also works well in conjunction with learning from a live teacher. If you want a more direct learning process and extra material, you can also order a video version of this course from the Zenways website.

Bits and pieces of these meditation practices have been previously translated into English but, to my knowledge, no one has put them together in a practical format. In that sense this book is a first. Each chapter aims to give you what is needed to fully engage in the practice under consideration so that it works for you. I recommend taking a week over each piece of the puzzle before working on the next one. As we go you'll also find links to a dedicated private website with audio and visual guidance.

Let's look at the practicalities.

WHAT YOU NEED AND WHAT YOU DON'T

In order to make a success of this work, *you need to really want to do it*. That's the primary and essential qualification.

The formal meditation period is 25 minutes a day, every day, over eight weeks – no more and no less.

Then take five minutes to write in a meditation diary. What do you write? Primarily treat this as a brain dump, putting down whatever occurs to you in the context of your previous 25-minute meditation experience. This serves a number of very useful purposes; chief among them is that it gives you a bit of distance and perspective on any emotional and mental material that may have arisen. Over time it's useful to go back and note particular themes and threads that recur.

In addition you can use the meditation diary to consciously track your progress in certain areas. We'll mention how to do this when we look at daily life practice in Chapter 9. I recommend you practise seven days a week, even if you have to squeeze time in other areas of your life.

There really is no substitute for the actual practice. It can be useful to read and study, but as Shinzan Rōshi frequently used to say, 'A picture of a rice cake won't fill your belly.'

You don't need to take on board any particular belief system or worldview. There are reams of philosophy and theory behind this work, but none of it is of use without the grounding in practice. Again, Shinzan Rōshi used to say, 'It is more important what you do than what you believe.'

If you suffer from schizophrenia, paranoia or other problems of this kind, you need very particular help for this work to be useful to you. Don't try to learn it out of a book. I recommend the work of psychiatrist Dr Russell Razzaque (https://twitter. com/mindfulrussell), who has been working with me on bringing some of these methods into the mental health arena. Help is there if you need it.

And that's it. You need nothing else. If you have the time to invest – 30 minutes a day for eight weeks – and if you're not suffering from serious mental health problems, we can set sail!

PART I

THE FIRST
FORTY-NINE DAYS

CHAPTER 1

THE PHYSICALITY
OF ZEN PRACTICE

Meditation's a mental business, right? That's what I originally thought.

When I first came to Zen practice, more than 25 years ago, I had recently run a marathon and thought I was pretty fit. I arrived at the Soto Zen[1] monastery and was duly instructed to fold myself into the cross-legged position and face a wall.

'Just sit there,' they said. 'Relax. Don't try to think or do anything.'

I was amazed. I had no idea how uncomfortable sitting still could be! My legs, my back, my shoulders – everywhere was tight. The whole experience was dominated by pain.

Somehow I stayed with it. I was taught some Zen yoga moves that helped my body to begin adapting.

In meditation, I did my best to stay present with these tight sensations. Over time the knots began to shift. My body

---

1   There are two major traditions in Japanese Zen. The Soto school emphasises sitting in openness; the Rinzai school has a similar practice we explore later, but also works in meditation with a spiritual question or *koan*.

adapted, and gradually I found my hips could open up, my shoulders could drop a little, my legs could release.

But as these areas opened, all kinds of memories, painful feelings and emotions came up. This physical and emotional release raged in my system for several years, and still continues somewhat.

Allowing this opening can, especially in the early stages, be a fearful thing to do. You really don't know what you are going to meet, but you're pretty sure it is not going to be pleasant. Is it worth going through this spiritual detox? Emphatically yes!

You may wonder if you have the courage to do this, but I can assure you that, if you really want to do this work, you can. Also, to a great degree, you can set the pace. If it's all feeling too much, just scale back your practice by shortening your sitting period.

And all of this opening up comes simply from doing your best to sit upright, relaxed and grounded in your position.

In Soto Zen they have a saying: 'Correct deportment is the Buddha *dharma*.'[2] Your physicality is considered that important.

The more you can transfer the elements of your sitting alignment into your daily life, from walking to the bus, to washing up, to lying in bed, the more rapidly this process of release can go on. Consequently, the more unburdened and free your life becomes.

We'll come back to this detox process shortly, but first, let's look at the practical aspects. How do you align your body for *zazen*, sitting Zen meditation practice?

---

2   The Buddha's truth.

ALIGNING YOUR BODY FOR ZEN PRACTICE

Even if you're very flexible, start by sitting on an upright chair with a flat base, as shown in Figure 1.1. This allows you to concentrate on developing the relaxed uprightness of the upper body. What happens with your legs is secondary. We'll look at other positions once we've got the essentials right.

Don't think that a chair is for inferior practitioners! The first Japanese Zen master resident in the USA, Sokei-an (1882–1945), had his students sit in chairs throughout his teaching career.

Settle the body. Ideally the hips are a little higher than the knees and the feet separated and flat on the floor. You may find it helpful to sit on a cushion to create something of a wedge shape beneath you. Your seat and your feet together give you the stability of a triangular base.

Figure 1.1: Sitting on a chair

Just for a moment, sit on your hands and feel your ischia (sitting bones) – two projections that will press downwards. It is through these that your weight transfers downwards most efficiently. Now, move your hands to your lap, lengthen your spine and the back of your neck, and sway your body a little in all directions, gradually settling into the sweet spot where your body lifts up out of your ischia with minimal effort.

As you find this balance point, allow your body to become still. Relax your shoulders. Keep your neck long and your head balanced weightlessly. Find your chin placement by imagining you are holding a soft ball to your chest underneath your chin – your chin is tucked slightly but your throat remains open.

Look down the length of your nose with a soft gaze towards the floor in front of you. You can lower your eyelids to the half-open position, or you can allow them to softly close. Some Zen teachers are very insistent that the eyes must be open. Shinzan Rōshi never was. In my own experience I'd say there are certain areas in meditation that you'll only ever explore with the eyes closed and certain areas that you'll only ever explore with the eyes open. Over time it's helpful to experience both.

Keep your mouth closed if you can, with the tongue broad and resting at the most comfortable place on the roof of your mouth. Allow your whole body to relax. Become aware of the rising and sinking of the natural breath, but maintain a gentle quality of muscle tone in your lower abdomen.

You are physically in the right place when you combine a sense of relaxation with balance and poise. Don't worry if it takes some time to achieve this, just do your best. As long as you have a human body and mind, there will always be some physical niggles. If you have any physical disabilities, just do what you can to find ease and openness in your posture.

> Initially you may find that you need to lean on the back of the chair, but don't let this take you out of line and, if possible, gradually train yourself to sit upright without any support.

If you find it helpful to work with an audio commentary explaining what you've just read, you'll find one online at www.zenways.org/practical-zen-online (the password is 'insight').

Some Zen practitioners claim that the whole of Zen is in the posture. For example, Suzuki Rōshi writes: 'Enlightenment is not some good feeling or some particular state of mind. The state of mind that exists when you sit in the right posture is, itself, enlightenment.'[3]

I'm sure that Suzuki Rōshi wasn't a physical perfectionist, however. We work with where we are. I knew a fine Zen master who was born with a severe curvature of the spine. Daito (1235–1308), one of the greatest of the early Japanese Zen masters, had a crippled leg and could only assume a full cross-legged position on his deathbed. Many of us, too, are likely to do our most profound meditation on our deathbeds. At that point, I doubt our posture will be anything special. Nevertheless, considering *zazen* (Zen meditation practice) as a profoundly physical activity has some important ramifications.

I started planning this book at the beginning of the Chinese year of the dragon. The dragon is an interesting symbol shared

---

3   Suzuki, S. (1970) *Zen Mind, Beginner's Mind* (edited by Trudy Dixon). New York: Weatherhill, p.26.

by the Eastern and Western worlds, but we have a significant and important difference across our cultures in how we relate to it.

In England we think of Saint George going out to fight, conquer and ultimately kill the dragon. By contrast, a common image in East Asia is of sages or Zen masters actually riding on dragons. So what is going on here, and what does this difference tell us?

One way of understanding these images is to consider that they represent a difference in our attitude towards nature, and particularly the body. In the Eastern interpretation, the dragon represents the body's life energy – a fierce and powerful force capable of exerting power over us. Here, in the Western world, particularly through the influence of Plato and the Greek schools of philosophy, the body is typically viewed as an animal or lesser thing that needs taming, and from which the spirit needs to find release. It is completely in accord with this view of physicality that a hero would go out and slay the dragon to bring about freedom.

But in Zen we don't kill the dragon. We don't kill anything. We learn how to come face-to-face with the dragon and with every part of our humanity. Sometimes this means looking into the dark.

You probably have areas within your history and your sense of self that are hard to face; perhaps there are regrets and shame. When we turn towards Zen practice and allow the consequent opening up to start, we begin to shine a light into all these dark corners. 'Turning the light around' was one of the ancient terms used for Zen practice.

Most of us have a long history of closing down or hiding these areas because life can then carry on in its regular routine with the illusion of safety. But if we just lock ourselves down, nothing is ever resolved. We become stuck.

It is true that what we find in the darkness may have a fearsome face, an evil dragon's face; there are aspects of your being that are profoundly antisocial. You may find aggression and powerful hatred. You may find urges that would repel normal, polite society. But in your practice, you simply provide a safe space for these feelings to arise.

Of course, it's important that you don't act on these feelings and emotions. An important safeguard is the ethical framework of the Zen precepts. So what do we do when negativity arises?

This is easy to explain but not necessarily easy to do. The Zen term *nari kiru*, which can be translated as 'become one with', is helpful here. It means we utterly accept the reality of the present moment – all of it. Your awareness provides the safe place where these feelings can arise. You don't hold on to them. You let the feelings come; you let them stay as long as they wish; you let them go. Let them come; let them go. When you're doing this correctly, even very strong feelings might arise and nobody around you would necessarily know what was going on. Although these feelings and emotions aren't suppressed, you aren't investing in them or acting them out. You simply provide the space where they can release.

In doing this, you begin to realise just how much effort and energy it takes to hold all these tensions inside. And, as the feelings liberate, all their bound-up energy becomes available for use in your life.

As a Zen practitioner, your job is to allow this physical softening and release of feelings to happen continuously; but even while this is happening, you still deal with the responsibilities in your life. Whatever you need to do, whether it's a business meeting with colleagues or playing with your children in the park, all this old stuff from the past just floats on through you. You let it all come – you let it go – let it come – let it go. That's it.

In the Zen monastery, life is set up so you have to do this. There is no choice. For the first seven years of my own practice I, like everyone else, had six foot by three of living, sleeping and meditation space on a platform in the meditation hall, and was almost never alone. We each had to deal with anger, frustration, sorrow or whatever else arose, without it spilling out onto others. There was nowhere to hide, no way to avoid it – we just had to deal with it.

When we do this work, we are putting into practice the way of compassion (from the Latin *com*, 'with', *passion*, 'pain'). However it manifests, we are willing to be with the pain, without running away and without closing it down.

In doing this, the dragon changes from being our enemy to becoming our vehicle. We learn to ride it, and enjoy life in all its power and glory. The rejected impulses that were thrust into the darkness become forces for good when transformed by our compassion.

This process of working with our physical posture underlies all the practices in this book and continues through life. You may well find that practising Zen yoga helps the opening. For now, spend all the time you need to get into a relatively comfortable and sustainable meditation position. As you begin to practise, you may find holding stillness for 25 minutes is not yet possible for you. Do what you can. When you need to move, do so, but maintain your awareness throughout.

CHAPTER 2

WORKING WITH THE BREATH

Shinzan Rōshi once gave me a calligraphy of the character *nen* or 'mindfulness' (see Figure 2.1). Like many characters, this is made up of two simpler ones. In this case the character for 'now' is placed above the character for 'heart' or 'mind'. When we practise mindfulness we're applying this present-moment mind, this present-moment attention to reality.

Figure 2.1: Calligraphy of the character nen by Shinzan Rōshi

As you sit here reading this book, take a moment to bring your attention to your breath. Where can you sense it most readily? Is it rough or smooth? Is there a quality of ease, or do you find tensions within the breathing process?

You'll notice, of course, that the breath constantly changes. In bringing your attention to the breath, you're necessarily bringing your attention to the present moment. So how does this present-moment awareness change things, both within your body and mind, and within your global experience?

You may find that this awareness causes you to let go of unnecessary tensions. You may find that your sensory experience is more vivid – perhaps the actual colour of the page is more vibrant, the feeling of your clothes on your skin, smells... You may be more aware of your prevailing mood. Is there an underlying disquiet or a sense of happiness? Perhaps, most important of all, you may notice that the sense of change you experience with the breath is actually present elsewhere too, even in seemingly solid things.

Even as you continue to read, allow this expanded awareness to persist. Within the Zen tradition, meditation on and with the breath has made much use of this effect.

When I first started meditating on the breath, I became aware of layers of muscular tension in the abdomen that prevented the flow of breath from penetrating very deeply. It was uncomfortable to maintain this awareness, and my mind constantly wanted to flit off into other areas. When I persisted, however, the layers of abdominal tension began to lift, and with them layers of embodied stress. My whole perspective on myself and life subtly shifted. My body restructured and the centre of gravity shifted downwards. For me this is still work in progress.

Breath practice can take us a long way. Shinzan Rōshi often pointed a direction to where breath practice can go. He would say, 'Breathe in the entire universe; breathe out your entire self.'

In Japanese, the meditation practice of counting the breath is called *susokukan*. Lay Zen master Eizan Tatsuta (1893–1979) wrote:

> *Susokukan* breath counting is designed to free you from eternal slavery to your emotions and keep your mind and body in a balanced state. Whenever you practise it you will reach a state of great calmness, will not be bothered by trivialities and be able to make rapid decisions in response to events which will help you to protect yourself in an emergency.[1]

It is the first meditation practice we're exploring because it is often the first one you encounter when starting Zen training. The simple human function of breathing has several ramifications for Zen practice. We'll begin to examine these by considering the two complementary categories of practice that Zen master Hakuin called the 'two wings of a bird'.

In the first category are meditation methods called *rikan* in Japanese. These practices help you to look into the heart of things, into reality itself. The second category or 'wing' is called *naikan* – practices designed to develop your health, your wellbeing, your groundedness and your power. Hakuin considered both to be essential for a successful practice that can be applied in a realistic way in the world. Working with the breath touches both aspects.

---

1   Tatsuta, E. 'A Guide to Susokukan Breath-Counting Meditation in Zen.' Available at www.ningenzen.org/lay.html#a1.1.4, p.1.

Let's look at the *naikan* aspect. How is paying attention to your breathing good for you? First, bringing your mind to the breath is a practice of bringing your mind to *something*. You can think of the mind as a muscle. Exercise makes it stronger. The experience of the mind flying off on tangents of distraction is pretty universal. An untrained mind simply won't stay long where you put it. Without the ability to sustain focus in a particular direction, it's very hard to achieve any real success in life. Using this very simple natural function of the breath, you can put in the time in the mental gym to develop this strength of mind.

In Zen I've encountered two broad approaches to this mental strengthening with breath meditation, each with particular benefits. Likening them to camera settings, I often think of them as narrow-focus and broad-focus.

In the narrow-focus meditation, we are drawing the attention exclusively to the breath. Every time a thought arises you immediately snip it off like a flower from a bush. Initially I found this maddeningly difficult! Over time, though, the focus builds and you begin to taste periods of exquisite quiet, incredible peace and bliss. A quite well-known approach in Japan has the student mentally count the in-breaths and out-breaths from 1 to 100. When you can make it right through to 100 three times without a single thought arising, you are considered to have mastered the practice. You might want to try it some time. Not now, however – we have other priorities. This narrow-focus breath meditation certainly strengthens the mind and potentially feels good. There are, however, limitations.

These days, the financial services industry is a huge influence on the City of London. Many of the people who have come to me since I have been teaching in London have been bankers. So many of them hate their jobs. Of course, the banking function is absolutely essential in modern society. Nevertheless, the stereotype of the stressed-out banker has entered the London consciousness. So I often talk about the contrast in breath focus as described below.

Imagine a banker who hates his job, has a horrible boss and has to work longer hours than is really sustainable. Nevertheless, he or she is making pretty good money. Because of this income our banker can afford to take a wonderful luxury holiday once a year, perhaps to a paradise island, where the climate, scenery and atmosphere are incredibly relaxing. During this week it's possible to completely forget about London, and all the stresses and strains, and deeply recharge and gather strength. After the holiday, however, it's back to the office, back to the boss, back to the grim day-to-day. Perhaps by the following Wednesday, the holiday is just a distant memory and a fading suntan.

Now, think of another banker. Rather than heading off to paradise, he or she stays around, has the difficult conversation with the boss, faces the unpleasant reality of life and starts to make some changes. This process will be far less sweet than the luxury island experience. However, over time, the changes will affect life every single day.

This is how the broad-focus approach to meditating with the breath works. As you sit in meditation, the centre of your attention is the breath, but now, rather than cutting off thoughts, feelings and perceptions, you simply allow them to arise and pass. Whenever you become distracted and lose your breath focus, you gently come back.

This approach builds your ability to concentrate, but it does something else as well. Because your focus is open, you become more directly aware of the changeable nature of your internal universe. The narrow-focus approach deliberately excludes greater and greater areas of reality; in this broad-focus approach everything is allowed – neither suppressed nor indulged.

Why is this significant? From the *rikan* point of view – the investigation of reality – the more directly we perceive the changeability of things, the more we naturally let go. This letting go is the gateway to liberation.

This broad-focus style of practice may make you feel better – it can change your *state* (but likely not so powerfully as the narrow-focus way). But it can also change your perception and consequently make you a different person – a change of *trait*. One of my teachers told me that the Zen tradition regards this as the practice that led the Buddha himself to enlightenment.

Because of this double benefit, and because it's far easier for beginners, I recommend the broad-focus approach.

We have some very ancient teachings from the Buddha on working with the breath. One definitive text in this context is called the *Mahasatipatthana Sutta* (literally, *The Great Discourse on the Foundations of Mindfulness*; see the translation at the beginning of Chapter 13). Among other practices, it highlights the work of *anapanasati*. *Ana* means 'out-breath', *pana* means 'in-breath', and *sati* means 'mindfulness'. So this text gives in-depth teachings on mindfulness of the in-breath and the out-breath. The Buddha taught that, by looking closely and clearly at the process of breathing, we can gain a deep insight into how things are. By looking at this one thing in detail, you can actually come to realise the truth of everything. The breath is very suitable for this kind of insight practice because the breath, by its very nature, is changing, moving and shifting.

So how does this work? The unexamined view of the self is that we are solid, a thing. We might feel like a billiard ball rolling across the table of life. Through meditation practice it becomes vastly easier to see that this is not how we are at all. Rather than being a thing in a world of things, we are a process in a world of processes. As we start to directly experience this dynamic reality, we find happiness. We'll discuss this in much more detail later.

As we know, the breath can be something that happens all by itself. It is mostly under the control of our autonomic nervous system and goes on whether we are aware of it or not. But it is also something we can bring under our voluntary control, so it crosses both sides of our nervous system: the voluntary and the involuntary.

In his teaching, the Buddha describes observing when 'a short breath is short and a long breath is long'. In other words, no attempt is made to manipulate the breathing in any way; we are simply present and aware in the process of breathing.

Our particular school of Zen also incorporates another aspect of breathing. Hakuin's *naikan* practices that we referred to earlier utilise the breath to build health, power and strength, and from this perspective there are good and bad ways to breathe. Both good and bad breathing could be a focus of mindfulness, and in that sense could lead to liberation, but for building your health there is definitely a beneficial way to breathe.

It is unfortunate that beyond the scientific aspects of exchange of oxygen and carbon dioxide, the function of breathing is not something that we learn about in early life. It would make a huge difference if society had even a basic understanding of its complexity, which goes far beyond gas exchange and physiology.

An osteopath I know tells me that almost 100 per cent of the people who come to him for physical realignment breathe in an unhealthy way, and his first task is always to teach people how to breathe.

You may well be wondering what it means to breathe incorrectly. Let's first consider the structure of the lungs. They are like a pair of balloons encased within the rib cage, which is itself similar in size and shape to a birdcage. The bottom of the rib cage (the floor of our birdcage) is a sheet muscle called the diaphragm, and between the ribs are other muscles called the intercostals.

Putting it simply, we can breathe in two ways. The intercostal muscles can pull the rib cage upwards to make space for fresh air to fill the top of the lungs, and the diaphragm at the base of the rib cage can drop to create space towards the bottom of the lungs.

Humans are unusual among mammals in that we walk upright, which means that the front surface of the body is exposed to the world. The upper part of our trunk is protected by the ribs and thus relatively safe, but the area of the abdomen below the ribs is soft and vulnerable. When humans feel threatened, stressed or under pressure, there is an automatic tightening of the muscles in the belly to protect this region. This tightening can include the diaphragm muscle. When the muscles of the abdomen and diaphragm are in a state of tautness, the diaphragm can't drop down to allow air into the lungs. Breathing is then left to the intercostal muscles moving the rib cage to allow air in and out of the top of the lungs. Breathing feels and actually does become shallow. So when we feel under pressure or stressed, we tend to only breathe into the top of the lungs.

This type of breathing can easily become a habit. Even in a totally relaxed situation, these shallow breaths continue. In this case, the body interprets this type of breathing to mean it is under stress and so releases stress hormones to prepare for emergency action. Blood is diverted into the heart, the brain and limbs – the areas concerned with immediate survival. Shallow breathing is therefore both a response to stress and a trigger for the body's stress response – a self-perpetuating harmful circle.

This stress response has evolved to help you deal with immediate danger. But when you're exposed to stress hormones over long periods of time, you typically end up with poor digestion, a feeling of jumpiness and instability, and an over-reaction to normal situations. Cold and clammy hands and feet may develop, and constipation and sexual dysfunction are very common. So a remarkably wide range of problems can be caused simply by bad breathing habits.

The converse is also true. When the breathing is relaxed and diaphragmatic, you feel good. Less stress hormones enter your bloodstream, which benefits digestion, elimination and other regulatory functions. Your whole system works so much better. So when we think about breathing and meditation practice, and also breathing to develop wellbeing, we need to get the diaphragm working.

When the diaphragm is working well and can move down to draw breath in, the pressure in the abdomen increases and the belly swells. As a result, when breathing in with your diaphragm, you can feel your belly expand. On the out-breath, when your diaphragm moves up or relaxes, you can feel your belly release. Our first job, then, as we learn to breathe correctly and to sort out our health and wellbeing on the breathing level, is to mobilise the abdomen.

Typically in the Zen school, when we are practising breath meditation, we rest our attention on the lowest place in the body where we can feel the sensations of movement. We don't try to manipulate the breath. It may be that, when we start, the breath is predominantly up in the chest. But simply by putting our attention low down and noticing what sensations are there in the moment, abdominal tightness gradually begins to unlock, and open diaphragmatic breath begins.

Other schools of meditation use different techniques. For example, one approach focuses on the feeling of the breath in the nostrils. This sensation is easy to feel and may help focus attention, but it does not encourage healthy abdominal breathing. This first step of practice, then, where we focus our attention on the breathing in the belly, helps to get the diaphragm working, and this in itself can potentially give you years more life.[2]

Once you establish this abdominal breathing within your practice, you will notice a couple of further developments. The first is that it becomes your signature or default breathing pattern. This is good, but there may be a downside: some people develop a belly bulge. Not only is this an undesired body shape, but it can occasionally lead to an exaggerated arch in the lower spine and some lower back pain.

We have a way of dealing with this. First, make sure your diaphragm is working, and there is a clear and comfortable sense of the belly expanding and releasing. Now find the muscles right at the base of your belly and very lightly lift and engage them. Doing this slightly tucks in your coccyx, or tailbone, which helps the lower spine to straighten rather than over-arch. With this little muscular tuck, your breathing is still definitely powered by the diaphragm, but your lower back and sides will expand and release as well as your belly.

---

2   See, for example, Chaitow, L., Gilbert, C. and Morrison, D. (2013) *Recognizing and Treating Breathing Disorders*, 2nd edn. Edinburgh: Churchill Livingstone.

It is important to stress that the diaphragmatic breathing should be properly established before you start adding muscle tone into the abdomen. Many people already have far too much muscle tension in this area, which needs to be released before anything else.

A further development from abdominal breathing is in the power and strength in the body. In Japanese, the abdomen is called the *hara*. When the *hara* is empowered, the whole body is empowered. Zen master Hakuin says that, when this area is really strong, it feels as though you have an inflated football in your belly. This is not bloating, but more a feeling of springy resilience.

This strength begins to develop when the diaphragm is working and you are able to get the little tuck in the lower belly. These two steps come first. Then you just sink your awareness, the centre of your attention, into your belly. You'll know you're doing it right when you feel a kind of openness in your head and softness in your chest together with the grounded, empowered sense in the belly.

There is a little spot three fingers' width below the navel right in the centre of your body. In Japanese this is called *tanden* (literally, 'elixir field'). This is the epicentre of your *hara*. If you can rest your attention here as you breathe, your practice will be particularly centred and powerful. Developing the *hara* is such an important subject in Zen that we will focus on it in a lot more detail in Chapter 6, but for now, the above pointers will hopefully get you started.

As mentioned earlier, *anapanasati* is the traditional name for 'mindfulness of the breathing'. *Pana* or *prana* is also the name, within the traditional Indian system of energetics, for the rising energy within the body. *Ana* refers to the energy that tends to sink within the body. So mindfulness of the breath can cross over into mindfulness of the vitality or energy within your system. We'll explore this later, too.

Also, as your practice develops, you'll begin to notice a very strong link between your breathing and your thought patterns. As your awareness becomes more refined, you may begin to notice how particular kinds of thought have associated kinds of breath. There are many kinds of breath, just as there are many kinds and densities of thought. Over time you may well find that thoughts start to die away. As the thoughts thin out, the breathing tends to become softer and lighter. You may even come to the point where there is no thought at all. The breath also disappears. There can be periods when it seems your whole being is just hanging in space. There is no breathing, no thinking; you are completely comfortable. You might go on like this for minutes at a time.

Typically, after a while you think, 'I haven't taken a breath for ages', and, of course, with that thought, the breath comes back immediately! This is territory you may find yourself exploring. It is absolutely fine and perfectly safe. Just because your breathing dies away sometimes, it doesn't signify that you are enlightened or special, so don't read too much into it. Equally, it's okay if that never happens.

You are not trying to stop the flow of thoughts and feelings here; you are not stopping anything at all. You simply allow the breath to be your focus and allow everything else to flow on through. Sometimes thoughts come in clouds, sometimes it's very quiet, but either way, you just stay with the breath. Of course, sometimes you get distracted and go off on trains of thoughts or feelings. But as soon as you notice this is happening, simply come back again to the breathing and counting. Let's try this in practice.

BREATHING MEDITATION

When you first come to learn meditation practice in a Rinzai Zen temple, you usually work with your breath. The Buddha teaches us that mindfulness, or awareness of the breath, can take us all the way to enlightenment, so don't think of this as just beginners' work.

Slowly read over these instructions. Take your time to familiarise yourself with what you're going to do. You can find a recorded audio version of these instructions online at www.zenways.org/practical-zen-online (the password is 'insight').

We're going to try to practise for 25 minutes. Set a timer. Intend to sit still. If you need to move occasionally, then do so. Nothing needs to be forced.

Adopt your meditation position. Whether sitting on a chair or the floor, you want to create a stable triangular base with your lower body. Make sure your knees are separated and the weight of your upper body is supported by your ischia, the two sitting bones in the base of your pelvis. Sway a little from side to side, forwards and backwards, to find your position of natural uprightness. Your spine should adopt its natural curves.

Relax your shoulders; have your neck long with the top of your head directly above your sitting bones. Rest your hands in your lap, on a cushion if necessary. Have your mouth closed with your tongue resting gently on the roof. Allow your eyes to lower, or if you wish, you can close them.

Relax your body. Allow your breathing to be natural.

Draw your attention to the breath. You may feel it in your belly or perhaps higher up in your body.

However low in the body you can feel your relaxed breath is the place for you to bring your attention. If you can feel your breath right down in the belly, rest your attention in your *tanden*, the little spot in the centre of your body about three fingers' width below the navel. Tune into the feeling of the rising and sinking.

Begin to mentally count your breaths. In-breath: one. Out-breath: two. In-breath: three. Out-breath: four. And so on, up to ten, when you begin again at one.

It's very simple: just breathing, just counting.

Allow thoughts, feelings and memories, anything at all, to arise and pass, but your focus point is simply the breath.

Any time you become distracted and lose count of your breath, just start again, counting in-breath: one; out-breath: two.

As your mind becomes more focused and concentrated, you may find your breath becomes light and gentle.

As your breath becomes more light and gentle, your body may become relaxed and comfortable.

It's very simple: just breathing and counting.

Sometimes you may find that meditation becomes more and more pleasurable, as you come into a state of restful clarity. And sometimes it won't feel that way. Whether thoughts and feelings arise, or whether things are very quiet, your meditation is equally valuable. All you do is stay with the breathing.

You may find, as your mind becomes more settled, that it's fine for you to just count your out-breaths: out-breath: one; out-breath: two; and so on all the way up to ten, and then beginning again at one.

As things go deeper still, you may even find you can drop your counting altogether and simply stay with the sensation of the breath: the rising and sinking. No counting, just pure awareness.

Or, if at any point you feel more distracted, as though you need a stronger anchor for your awareness, you can go back to counting your in-breaths and your out-breaths.

It doesn't matter which method is good for you; you may find different methods work well on different occasions. The important thing is to practise.

And as you come to the end of your meditation, gently sway your body side to side. Coming back slowly, allow your eyes to lift. Your meditation period is over.

If you are a new practitioner, I recommend you spend the first week practising on a chair. If you wish, you can keep going like this throughout the rest of the practices in this book.

Work with this practice 25 minutes a day, every day, for a week. At the end of each period, remember to spend five minutes writing in a meditation diary. Treat this as a brain dump. Just write down whatever comes to mind for five minutes, close the book, and get on with your life. As mentioned, the meditation diary is a very helpful way of integrating and making sense of your developing meditation experience.

Also note down in your diary a guesstimate of what percentage of the time you can stay with the breath awareness as opposed to getting distracted into trains of thoughts or feelings.

At first, and perhaps during the particularly busy times in your life, you may find you need to count your in-breaths and your out-breaths throughout this practice to help you stay focused. However, once you can stay with the counting about 80 per cent of the time, this might be the time to switch to counting the out-breaths. Here we are again mentally counting from one to ten, but we've reduced the strength of the anchor for our concentration.

If you stay with counting only the out-breath for a while, you'll reach a point where again you can maintain your undistracted focus for about 80 per cent of the time. This might be the time to explore dropping the counting altogether and just follow the feeling of the breath. Simply be aware when a short breath is short and when a long breath is long. It is very simple.

Everyone is different. Some people can concentrate very easily and some need a bit more training. If ever you feel you need to work in a more focused way to develop your concentration skills, the counting can be extended, as mentioned previously.

Although in this work our central focus is the breath, there may be times when persistent thoughts or feelings arise. Then it's best to switch your focus from the breath to the thought or feeling. Don't try to change it or make it go away; just be with it. This awareness will enable it to resolve. Then go back to your breath.

It is important to note here that a central element of this mindfulness practice is its non-manipulative nature. There is nothing to be gained from getting cross with yourself when your thoughts wander away from your breathing. We are not trying to change anything; we are just seeing how things really are. And it this clear seeing that opens the door to liberation.

UNCOVERING YOUR FUNDAMENTAL ADEQUACY

The Unborn

Just for a moment put your attention right in the centre of your body in the point we mentioned previously – the *tanden* – at a level roughly three fingers' width below the navel in the very centre of your body. Rest here for a moment. Now allow your attention to expand to include your whole body, your mind and all the sensations and thoughts arising and passing. Now keep expanding outwards. Allow your awareness to include all the sounds and sights in your environment. Keep expanding further until there's no limit, no sense of an edge.

Now let go of the central point – the *tanden*. Notice how there can be awareness without a fixed centre. You simply let go and allow. Any time you become aware of any holding on, just let go.

If you can, stay here for a few minutes. If it seems impossible, don't worry; just do your best.

Perhaps you can continue reading but still maintain this spaciousness. How would that be?

This utterly simple practice involves no strain or effort. Shinzan Rōshi calls it 'the easy way of Zen'. Simply rest into the present moment. Many Zen people practise this way. I did myself for well over a decade. There is nowhere you need to go; the present reality is our true home.

Within this openness and acceptance, profound transformation happens – sometimes gradually, almost imperceptibly, sometimes powerfully. I remember once, when I was in my first year as a monk, sitting in the crowded meditation hall in this openness. Within me there was a quality of gathering, an energetic drawing in. Suddenly, utterly unexpectedly, there was an inner explosion. I was projected into a whole new, boundless realm of experience and power. There was nothing I could do. Turning it off was impossible; I could only surrender. I rose up from the sitting, ignited in a new way. From then on it was utterly clear that the commonplace sense of 'me' as a fixed, solid object, like a billiard ball rolling across the table of life, was laughably out of tune with reality.

I think the simplicity and surrender of this way of practice can teach us achievement-driven Westerners a great deal. One of my students, a financial consultant, said:

'It's been a profound shock to me to realise how so much of what I do has been based in a feeling that I'm not okay. I have to somehow earn my okay-ness. Again and again this practice brings me up against the ways that I don't allow myself to simply be just as I am. And when I drop all that: bliss. It's all right here waiting for me.'

Zen master Bankei, founder of Gyokuryuji (my home temple in Japan), was one of Japan's greatest Zen masters. He spent his life helping people from all walks of life to find and live from this fundamental adequacy.

When I arrived at Gyokuryuji, Shinzan Rōshi said to me, 'I am like a samurai, I have two swords in my belt: the sword of Bankei and the sword of Hakuin.' The teachings of these two Zen masters, Bankei and Hakuin, were his inspiration, and largely the inspiration behind this book.

Sitting over tiny cups of tea in the spring sunshine, not long after I arrived, I asked Shinzan Rōshi a question: 'Your own way of Zen study was the hard-style Hakuin practice with a *koan* [a spiritual question]. Why did you also want to promote Bankei's gentle teaching, which is so different?'

'It's different and not different,' he said.

It was some time later when he decided to say more. We were having tea again. We looked out over the raked gravel. Shinzan Rōshi had been weeding in the morning sunshine with the rest of us. (It was only much later that I realised how unusual it was in Japan to be able to talk so freely with a Zen master.)

'All Westerners are like Bankei Zenji,' he said. I was taken aback, not at all sure what he was pointing at. He then proceeded to show Bankei's heart through acting out his life. This is what he told me (supplemented by *The Unborn*, a translation of some of Bankei's teachings[1]).

Rinzai Zen master Bankei Yotaku (Figure 3.1) was born about 400 years ago in western Japan. This was during the period dominated by the samurai class, and he, himself, came from a low-ranking samurai family. The samurai class were the leaders of society, mostly involved in administration and defence. Bankei's father, however, was a doctor.

---

1   Waddell, N. (translator) (1984 [2002]) *The Unborn: The Life and Teachings of Zen Master Bankei*. San Francisco, CA: North Point Press.

Bankei, or Muchi as he was then called, was the second boy. From early life he was stubborn and independent with an enquiring mind – not at all the norm in Japan, then or now. His mother eventually found a way to get some control. When he was disobedient, she would pretend to die. She would scare him into being good. No doubt there was a psychological cost to this.

Muchi was a bright boy. At this time, a samurai-class boy's education was centred on the classics of Confucianism – the basis of Japanese civil society. These teachings, imported from China, encoded correct social relationships. It was laid down how a father should act towards his son, and how a student should relate to a teacher; every common relationship was codified. The boys studied this material in preparation for becoming rulers and leaders in society.

Figure 3.1: Zen master Bankei Yotaku

One of the Confucian classics he studied was the *Daigaku*, or the *Great Learning* or *Great Cultivation*. It opens with the statement, 'The man of great learning knows how to bring forth illuminating virtue, to harmonise the people, and to abide in the achievement of the good.'[2]

It was this first little phrase that really caught the boy's attention: he really wanted to understand 'how to bring forth illuminating virtue' (*myotoku* in Japanese).

---

2   Author's translation.

'What does it mean? How do you do that?' he asked his teacher. But the teacher just gave him the set, textbook answers. Muchi was not satisfied. He could tell the teacher's response had no basis in any real experience.

A yearning emerged in the boy. He really wanted to find this illuminating virtue. Shinzan Rōshi emphasised that the conscious mind's formulation of this yearning is different person to person. For you it might be: 'What is the meaning of life?' or 'How do I find happiness?' But the power of this yearning is something we share. It may be like an underground river; it may be right on the surface. It may be a little stream or a mighty torrent. But it is there. You have it. You wouldn't be reading this otherwise.

Those of us who engage in this spiritual adventuring always tap into this yearning and follow its current, and Muchi was no different.

After his daily Confucian schooling was an after-school calligraphy class. Mastery of the brush was another essential accomplishment for an educated gentleman. If you've ever struggled with dull and mechanical educational methods, you can imagine the torture Muchi went through in endlessly brushing the same characters. Muchi's way of dealing with the torment was to escape. The minute the teacher turned his back, he would be out the door and on his way home!

He would arrive home early and perhaps his mother would pretend to die. An illiterate son could bring disgrace on the family, so she really tried to persuade him to take his studies seriously, only to meet his stubbornness.

And then, when Muchi was about 11 years old, his father died. Suddenly his elder brother, at perhaps 13 or 14, was the head of the family. They were no doubt all in shock, and big brother was probably feeling very insecure in his new position. He took it on himself to get little brother in line.

Between the calligraphy school and the family house there was a river. A boat ferried travellers across. So big brother decided to bribe the ferryman to refuse the truant, hoping this would change his ways.

The following afternoon, Muchi showed up early, as usual. As arranged, the ferryman refused to take him. The boy said, 'Well, I'm sure the ground carries on under the river.' And he walked straight through it and arrived home, dripping wet. Big brother, furious, threw the disobedient boy out of the house. Muchi was disowned, and unwelcome. The boy had nowhere to go. His father was dead. He was homeless. Muchi's future and his life itself looked precarious.

Luckily, family friends a few miles away heard about the problem with Muchi's elder brother and took pity on the boy. They offered him a little hut on their property and he promptly moved in. This, it seems, became his little hermitage. Friends offered their support, so he had a food supply, and, liberated from his family's expectations, he no longer had to attend school.

So what did he do with his time? He still wanted to know. He was still searching for the truth: 'How does it all fit in? What's it all about?' He wasn't getting many answers but the questioning continued.

He lived up there for a couple of years and it seems he visited various Confucians and Buddhists in pursuit of his question. At some point someone said to him: 'You should take this up with the Zen people. They specialise in these difficult questions.' So he decided to head down to a Rinzai Zen temple about 40 miles away to see if anyone could help. He walked in and met Umpo, the Zen master.

Straight away, the boy asked the Zen master about this 'illuminating virtue' and how to bring it forth. The teacher told him, 'You'll only find it within. You need to practise *zazen*.'

He showed Muchi how to do it – very likely using the breath, as we did in the last chapter. Thus a way forward appeared.

The boy was taken with this new avenue and asked to become a monk. Umpo, clearly recognising his sincerity, agreed. So the boy dedicated himself to Zen practice pretty much there and then. Muchi moved into the temple, began his meditation practice, and learned the ways of monastic deportment. He stayed for a couple of years. It seems he also reconnected with his education in reading and writing. And then, when he was about 17, he decided to take off on a pilgrimage in search of a great, enlightened teacher who could put all of his problems to rest.

In your own life, perhaps you've found yourself looking for the perfect person, the one who will solve all your problems. Or perhaps you're one step ahead of Bankei and already know that looking for the answer from another person is looking in the wrong direction.

Anyway, Bankei headed off with great hopes and wandered all over Japan. He was dedicated and assiduous in his practice, visiting temples, interviewing teachers and sleeping rough or in little huts he found or made. He showed up back at his home temple four years later. In all that time he had not found a single teacher who could help him. Not one. He was extremely disappointed, literally weeping with frustration.

Umpo told him, 'Of course you haven't found what you're searching for. You're looking in the wrong direction.' He pointed to Bankei's heart. 'This is where you find the answers.' At last, Bankei got the message: he had to look within. He turned towards meditation, throwing all his considerable determination into the work. It was do or die now. There were no other options.

To further his quest he moved out of the temple and built himself a tiny hermitage in a place called Ako some way from the temple, and walled himself in. The door was sealed up with mud plaster. There was no way out. There was only a small opening at the front, like a letterbox, through which people could put food, and a hatch at the back for defecation.

Bankei stayed in the hut and just meditated and meditated, searching relentlessly within. In later years he told his students how this striving was misdirected effort. But at the time it was the best he knew. He became really sick with a lung problem, possibly tuberculosis. He grew weaker, but the illness meant nothing. He continued meditating. There was nothing else he could do. He just kept looking, looking, looking within, seeking for that which would resolve all his doubts. His strength declined. He was close to death.

At this point, according to the texts, he was in a very open state. Suddenly there was a shift. In his own words, 'I spat against a wall. A mass of black phlegm, large as a soapberry, rolled down the side... Suddenly just at that instant...I realised what it was that had escaped me until now. All things are perfectly resolved in the Unborn.' He was cured.

Later, the scent of plum blossom reached his nostrils and in that moment all obstacles and attachments were swept away. He got up, smashed his way out of the hut and declared: 'I feel better!' He had finally found what he had been looking for.

He was frail but able to march down the hill back to Zen master Umpo, who was delighted. However, in Zen it is not enough for there to be realisation; it has to be actualised, to be made real in lived experience. One way this can be worked on is through testing. So, after a recovery period, Umpo told Bankei to go and try out his understanding, meeting as many teachers as he could to see if he could take it deeper.

So Bankei went wandering on pilgrimage again, but this time he was a very different person, so the world looked very different too.

One night he was heading for a temple called Daisenji, seat of a famous master called Gudo. Bankei arrived at a marketplace. It was starting to get dark. It was obvious to everyone that he had nowhere to stay. He was miles away from any temple, so one of the farmers invited him to go back to his house to stay and have supper.

In the farmer's house the family sat around the hearth to eat, and the young monk joined them. And perhaps he had some kind of a peaceful quality or maybe there was a special shine in his eyes; whatever it was, the family sensed something special about Bankei. After eating, they asked him for some teaching. He very simply talked about his life, what he had found, and how others could find it too. Soon he dropped off to sleep on a mat by the fire.

But while he was asleep, the farmers held a midnight meeting with their neighbours and decided they wanted Bankei to be their monk. There was a little piece of land in the mountain up above the houses where about 100 years before there had been an earthquake that had flattened the terrain into a bowl shape. They could build something for him up there.

So, when Bankei woke up in the morning, they greeted him with this proposition and he agreed. The villagers built a little hermitage and he went up there to live. He called it Gyokuryuan: *gyoku* means 'pearl' or 'jewel', *ryu* means 'dragon', and *an* means 'hermitage' – 'hermitage of the dragon's jewel'. (This was later changed to Gyokuryuji, 'temple of the dragon's jewel'.) He was very happy up there and they were happy to have him.

Bankei became very popular. Word got out about the enlightened young Zen hermit and people started to visit – first in the tens, and then hundreds started to descend on the tiny village.

Not only did Bankei feel he was causing an inconvenience, he wanted to continue his own quest. He went to meet a recently arrived Chinese Zen master called Dosha, and for a while stepped out of the Japanese Rinzai school to study with him. More mountain hermitage time followed. Then he began to teach at the bigger temples in the cities.

Bankei's teaching attracted people because it was extremely simple and clear. As we'll see below, he put his energy into helping people to realise that they already had what they seek. He developed a unique way of helping people to find peace and satisfaction in their lives. Thousands came to him.

But even as his reputation grew, he kept in touch with the people from the village below Gyokuryuji, and would stay there when he could. Some years later the villagers organised a 90-day winter teaching meeting for Bankei.

He returned to Gyokuryuji for the retreat, and as many as 6000 people joined him. The temple was tiny and would have been completely overcrowded with 20 people, so this was an incredible feat.

Very soon after this meeting, in 1693, Bankei died. Descendants of the farmer who invited the monk to stay in the village, the Sugiyama family, still live below the temple where master Bankei gave his first and last public teaching. Many years later, Shinzan Rōshi restored Gyokuryuji and made the hermitage his teaching seat.

During his lifetime, Bankei encountered criticism and opposition. He says, 'When I was young and first began to declare the Unborn *dharma*, people had trouble understanding it. They thought I was preaching heresy or they took me for a Christian. They were afraid of me. No one would come near.'[3]

---

3   Waddell, N. (translator) (1984 [2002]) *The Unborn: The Life and Teachings of Zen Master Bankei.* San Francisco, CA: North Point Press, p.55.

Looking into the events of Bankei's life, Shinzan Rōshi felt a great affinity with the staunch independence and boundless kindness of the former Zen master. It was this sense of sturdy self-reliance in Bankei that Shinzan felt was akin to his Western students.

'Bankei helped many people,' he said. 'I wanted to do the same.' Shinzan took the unprecedented step of making Bankei's gentle teachings and the warrior intensity of Hakuin-style practice available simultaneously. Like Bankei, he came to be considered an independent-minded maverick.

No less an authority than the great Zen scholar Suzuki considered Bankei a spiritual genius. But what does this master have to offer us living amid the stresses and strains of modern life? To get some context on this, let us take a quick overview of two routes or models of spiritual development.

The first route supposes that you begin from a feeling that life is not how it could or should be. You sense that something is missing. Maybe you feel out of tune or miserable or alienated. The spiritual journey takes you from here, away from this nagging disharmony, all the way to fulfilment.

Success, according to this mindset, would be the sense that you have reached your goal. You now have purpose, meaning and value to your life. You find bliss and a sense of deep rightness. There is definitely a truth to this route of spiritual development, and many religions have this kind of journey at their core.

The other route or model is found within one of the key Buddhist teachings, the *Lotus Sutra*. This is perhaps the most all-embracing of the traditional Buddhist teachings. Many of the key teachings are expressed through stories and parables. One story describes a man who attends a party, and gets well and truly drunk. His best friend wants to make sure he is taken care of, but has to leave early the next morning before the drunken man has emerged from his stupor. To ensure he has all he needs, the friend sews a precious jewel into the sleeping man's cloak, and then he goes on his way.

Finally waking alone, the now sober man sets off wandering through the world feeling absolutely abandoned and bereft. He struggles through a hand-to-mouth existence until, eventually, meeting the old friend again, he realises that all the while he has been carrying this priceless jewel. He has had absolutely everything he needed right from the beginning.

How do we make use of these seemingly contradictory models? I recommend starting at the end. Consider how it would be if, right now, at this very moment, the jewel is here, in your cloak. You don't have to seek. It's all just a matter of settling into this place – the place Bankei Zenji liked to call the Unborn. He said we lose this place when we get lost in things such as our thoughts, feelings and views, and that all of these things arise and pass. They are all things that are born and die.

The Unborn isn't separate from any of these arising and passing things. But when we identify with this changing scenery, we get lost. So in this practice we simply allow ourselves to rest in the present by not going anywhere else. It is a process of trust.

You truly have everything from the beginning and all you need to do is to rest in this ungraspable centre. You can read more of Bankei's words in Chapter 13.

Many Westerners have encountered Zen through the Soto Zen practice of *shikan taza*, which can be translated as 'single-minded sitting'. How does this contrast with the Unborn teachings of Zen master Bankei? In practice there is much commonality; however, in his teaching Bankei doesn't particularly prioritise sitting over any other posture, rather stressing that we can rest in the Unborn throughout all our activities.

Let's explore master Bankei's way in practice. As mentioned in Chapter 1, you may wish to practise sitting on a chair (see Figure 1.1). If you wish, keep going like this. Or you might consider other options, as shown in Figure 3.2. All positions have the same alignment of the upper body.

Some practitioners prefer to sit on the floor. You can kneel in a position called *seiza* (in Japanese), with a support beneath your sitting bones and your knees separated to create a stable base (see Figure 3.2a). Some students like to use a cushion; others prefer a meditation bench. Whatever you use, the support should be low but sufficient to lift your buttocks from your heels. In this position it is important that your clothing is loose enough so there is no restriction of the blood supply in your legs.

Traditionally Zen practitioners sit cross-legged with a cushion to lift the sitting bones. In this case, having both knees resting down creates the stable, triangular quality. You may find it most comfortable to start with one lower leg placed in front of the other (see Figure 3.2b).

As you gain flexibility you may find you can draw up one ankle into the hip crease of the opposite leg and sit in the half-lotus position (see Figure 3.2c). Eventually you may be able to draw up both legs like this, into full lotus (Figure 3.2d). It is important, however, that you don't force anything, and take particular care with your knees.

Depending on the relative length of your arms and your upper body, you may find you need a little support for your hands in your lap. A small towel or something similar placed under your hands can lift them sufficiently to prevent any excess strain on your shoulders.

Figure 3.2: Floor-based zazen (meditation) postures:
(a) sitting in seiza on a meditation bench; (b) the Burmese position;
(c) the half-lotus position; (d) the full-lotus position

As you explore adopting these positions, gradually lengthen the time you hold them. Proceed gently without any strain. You might start with a few minutes and gradually extend until you are comfortable with 25 minutes or longer. Most of the practices we're going to explore are based in this position. As you explore applying them, be gentle. Move when you need to. Things will eventually settle into stillness. Don't force it.

You will notice that all these positions encourage uprightness combined with relaxation. This helps to foster mental clarity combined with ease.

Although sitting meditation is very important within our practice, it is not the only posture we focus on. The Buddha always talked of the four postures of meditation – sitting, standing, walking and lying down – and all of these are important. When we stand, we have the hips and shoulders in the same relationship as when we sit. We have the same alignment of the spine falling into its natural curves. When we walk, these elements are brought into motion, and when we lie down, we do the same again. Ideally there is an ongoing sense of alignment in the body.

UNBORN MEDITATION

As with the meditation with the breath, you may like to set a timer so you know when you have practised for 25 minutes.

Come into your sitting place, and read over these instructions slowly. Then put the book down and carry right on resting in this Unborn place. You can find a recorded audio version of these instructions online at www.zenways.org/practical-zen-online (the password is 'insight').

First get comfortable in your sitting place. You can sit on a chair with your feet planted firmly on the floor, or you can kneel with your sitting bones resting on a cushion or meditation bench. Or it may be that you prefer to sit cross-legged with a cushion beneath your buttocks.

Whichever is most comfortable, you want to create your stable triangular base with your lower body. Make sure your knees (or feet, if you're on a chair) are separated and the weight of your upper body is supported by your ischia, the two sitting bones in the base of your pelvis. Sway a little from side to side, forwards and backwards, to find your position of natural uprightness. Your spine should adopt its natural curves.

Relax your shoulders; have your neck long with the top of your head directly above your sitting bones. Rest your hands in your lap, on a cushion if necessary. Have your mouth closed with your tongue resting gently on the roof. Allow your eyes to lower, or if you wish, you can close them.

Relax your body. Allow your breathing to be natural. Feel the rising and sinking of the breath in your belly.

In this meditation practice you don't particularly focus on the breath. In fact, there is no particular focus on anything. You just do your best to stay 100 per cent present, regardless of whatever arises and whatever passes away.

It is this quality of presence that is the important thing.

Zen master Bankei wants you to sit like a mirror, allowing the arising and passing of thoughts, feelings, emotions, sounds: anything at all. You just stay in this mirror-like presence.

For now, you can just be. There is nothing to do, nothing to chase after.

The mirror never changes. Perhaps it reflects many things, perhaps only a few. None of them matter. All these arisings are born things and you rest in the Unborn.

The only task is to observe when you begin to identify with or attach to any of these born things. When you recognise this is happening, immediately you are resting again in the Unborn.

It is all very simple. You just rest in this quality of presence with this unborn mirror-like awareness.

In this place you lack for nothing. Just relax; enjoy the show. The arising and passing – none of it is you. In this place, you're quite safe, so anything at all can arise, and anything at all can pass, and you're absolutely fine.

In this place you are completely free. It is free space. Even these words pass across the great, round mirror of your awareness.

Here you can know that your unborn, absolutely indestructible Buddha nature is always present. Here, your unborn presence that encompasses all things comes to the forefront.

This small shift in perspective is all that's called for.

As your sitting meditation period comes to an end, and it's time to engage in other activities, take the opportunity to rest in this Unborn presence as much as you can. Allow things to arise and pass, and just deal with that which is necessary. How simple and straightforward can your life be? How clear and open and enjoyable can it all be?

As mentioned, from this Unborn perspective, spirituality is not really a quest. It is more about settling into your fundamental adequacy and living a life from the place that is based in this truth.

People who have this kind of spiritual understanding look around at everyone else and can see they, too, have it already.

We just need to unpick our cloaks a little, and here, right now, is the beautiful jewel.

So we don't need to particularly change ourselves or try to make ourselves into something else. We don't have to go on painful courses of practice or force ourselves in any way. This is about acknowledging the truth of who we are, who we were, and who we always will be.

Of course, both the 'spiritual quest' and the 'you're already there' models of development outlined previously are true: they represent different perspectives of the same thing. I like the saying, 'The opposite to a conventional truth is a lie, but the opposite to a profound truth is another profound truth.' Nevertheless, different teachers and different teachings tend to emphasise one facet or the other.

When Bankei instructed his students about this place of the Unborn, he said it had a quality of *reimei*. In Japanese, *rei* means 'spiritual' and *mei* means 'brightness' or 'illumination', so within you is a place of pure brightness that has nothing to do with external illumination. It is a place of deep power and deep satisfaction.

There are, of course, so many things that can pull you from here, so many forces in your life that may have convinced you that you're not really good enough or that on some level you don't have what you need. But at any moment you can settle back into this place and allow the consequent unfolding. It is all yours; it always was and always will be. When you rest in this place, even if only for a few moments, you lack for nothing.

When you come into this ungraspable place, Bankei taught, you are at the wellhead of all the Buddhas and all the Zen ancestors. You truly have within you, just as you are, the source. This place is the true centre of the universe, and to settle here is the work of a moment. There is actually nothing to it: arriving here is totally straightforward. You can do it right now.

The trick is to stay here. If you can allow yourself to rest in this place, not doing anything, not seeking anything, then a spiritual unfolding begins to happen. It can't be forced, just as a rose cannot be forced to open its petals. The unfolding happens all by itself.

Now you may be one of those people who can naturally and easily settle into the Unborn and allow this unfolding to occur. If so, you truly have nothing further to seek, and need only allow the process. Or it may be that this doesn't fully resonate with you yet, in which case you'll benefit from some of the other practices in this book to help you deal directly with all the extraneous stuff of life: the distractions, feelings of inadequacy, uncontrollable emotions and inability to make progress. And as we deal with this arising, or 'born', scenery, we find ourselves able to release more into the Unborn.

This place may not be obvious, at least at first. The old masters called it a place of 'thin gruel and weak tea'. It doesn't taste of much, and that is why it is so easy to get pulled out by the dramas of life. But if you allow yourself to become familiar with this thin flavour, over time, you'll find it deeply satisfying.

At first it is often easiest to rest in this ungraspable place during your *zazen* (sitting meditation). For the next week, spend 25 minutes a day sitting with this, followed by five minutes writing about your experience in your meditation diary.

It is important to understand, however, that the Unborn is actually here all the time, whatever you are doing. You can live here permanently and allow your whole life to flow out of this place.

Strangely enough, although this place has an ungraspable quality, an imperative for action rises out of it and, if we truly trust the process, the things that need to be done do actually get done. Somehow the decisions that need to be made get made. There is a harmonious, natural quality that is completely unfabricated.

Although we start at the destination with Bankei's approach, there is, nevertheless, a 'ripening'. He said:

> Upon confirming yourself in the Unborn, you acquire the ability to see from the place of that confirmation straight into the hearts of others. The name the Zen school is sometimes given, the 'Clear-eyed' sect, stems from this. There, at that place of confirmation, the Buddha's *dharma* is fully achieved. Once the eye that can see others as they are opens in you, you can regard yourself as having fully achieved the *dharma* because wherever you are becomes a place of total realisation. When you reach that place, no matter who you are, you are the true successor to my *dharma*.[4]

So, a prime characteristic of this opening is that you become able to see into the heart of the person standing in front of you. And when you know where they stand, you can be of genuine help.

Bankei Zenji stressed that this place of the Unborn is yours, regardless of what you are doing. He very much encouraged his students to explore what it means to get dressed in the Unborn, to walk down the street in the Unborn, to do your work in the Unborn.

It is entirely yours, it always was, and it always will be.

---

4   Waddell, N. (translator) (1984 [2002]) *The Unborn: The Life and Teachings of Zen Master Bankei*. San Francisco, CA: North Point Press, p.37.

CHAPTER 4

YOUR BURNING QUESTION

Meditating with a Koan

You have trained the mind, at least to a certain extent, by practising with your focus on the breath for a week. You've gone on to spend a week sitting in the pure, open spaciousness of the Unborn meditation. Both of these practices can lead to liberating insights. Now we're going to explore another way of insight: working with a spiritual question, a *koan*.

Just as you are right now, settle your body comfortably. Ask yourself internally, 'Who am I?' Really ask it. Ask again if you wish. Now simply be open. Notice whatever arises.

In this noticing, there may be all manner of things, thoughts, theories, memories, even profound silence. Simply notice.

Now ask: 'Who am I?' Again, be open.

And for a third time: 'Who am I?' Again, simply watch and be present with whatever comes up.

Let's look into this process of working with a *koan*. Even people with no knowledge or interest in Zen are aware of its association with confusing questions such as 'What is the sound of one hand clapping?' There are many such others:

- How do you put out the fire on the other side of a mountain?
- What is your original face before your parents were born?
- What is Buddha? Three pounds of flax.

A question or *koan* of this type is not a riddle or intellectual conundrum; it is a tool to bring forth your non-dualistic understanding, the place where you find a happiness that is not reliant on any external circumstances.

One of my teachers used to say that a *koan* is something that from the outside has no solution, but from the inside is no problem. Their use stretches back through the centuries. The practice continues because it works, and it's fast.

In his teaching, Bankei did not emphasise practising with *koans*. However, in his own life, the question of how to bring forth illuminating virtue occupied him for years and formed the basis of his life's work. Some *koans* arise naturally like this; others can be taken up by the conscious mind and thence tap into the underground river of our desire to awaken. Both ways work.

The word *koan* translates literally as 'public case', so it is a sort of legal term. Some people think of it as a judgment. In our legal system, a judgment in a case can set a precedent that from then on is taken into account in similar cases. A *koan* can be thought of as a precedent of enlightened expression.

At the beginning of this book we discussed how the world of suffering (*dukkha*) is a world of duality and conflict, whereas the world of peace and happiness is non-dual. The normal structures of adult language and thought reflect a profoundly dualistic way of relating to the world.

In contrast, the deliberately unorthodox or paradoxical use of words within *koans* helps us to enter the world of non-dualistic understanding. We resolve a *koan* by becoming one with a *koan*. The world of separation, of duality, is thus transcended and we find this other realm, the delightful place that is not split or alienated.

Shinzan Rōshi liked to say that he taught the Unborn Zen of Bankei and the *Koan* Zen of Hakuin. We know something about Zen master Bankei already, so what about Hakuin? This is what Shinzan Rōshi told me (supplemented by his autobiography *Wild Ivy*[1]).

Hakuin Ekaku (Figure 4.1) was born in 1689 and so was a little younger than Bankei. They never met. At this time, the two most important cities in Japan were Tokyo (or Edo, as it was then called) and Kyoto, the old capital. The road that connected them was called the Tokaido. Hakuin's family ran a coaching inn on this road close to the base of Mount Fuji, and he was brought up in this bustling environment. As a boy he developed an overpowering dread of death and hell.

To try to find some peace from this fear, he left home at 14 and became a Zen monk at the tiny temple in his village. He was an intelligent boy, sincere and earnest.

There was a Zen training monastery a few miles from his home base. But when he arrived, Hakuin found to his

---

1   Waddell, N. (translator) (2010) *Wild Ivy: The Spiritual Autobiography of Zen Master Hakuin*. Boston, MA: Shambhala Publications Inc.

disappointment that the monks were focused on studying Chinese poetry rather than meditation. He gave up on his aspiration for a while, joining in with the study, but the dread in his heart would not leave him alone for long. So he left the temple and travelled on in search of a teacher who could help him on his quest.

In his wanderings he could not find any good teachers. After some time he ended up in a temple called Eiganji and decided to make the journey on his own. He was attending a study meeting, but he took himself into a secluded little shrine, locked himself in and practised *zazen*, sitting and a sitting focusing on the *mu koan*.[2]

On the seventh day, deep in his meditation, he heard a distant bell ringing. He had a tremendous *kensho* (enlightenment experience) and walked out of the shrine, convinced that he was the most realised person for hundreds of years, and that nobody could even approach his level of understanding. At the time, there was no one around to contradict him. In his autobiography, Hakuin describes how his pride was the size of a mountain.

By sheer good fortune he met a monk called Sokaku. This monk told him of his

Figure 4.1: Zen master Hakuin

---

2 The *mu koan* concerns an encounter in which a young monk came to Zen master Joshu and asked, 'Does a dog have the Buddha nature?', to which the master replied, 'Mu.' This *mu* literally means 'no' or 'not', but in this case is beyond affirmation or denial.

own teacher, the hermit Shoju Rojin,[3] who lived near the village of Iiyama, to the north. Hakuin was curious to meet Shoju, and accompanied Sokaku to visit the teacher. As he arrived, Hakuin's pride in his attainment was obvious. He requested an interview with Shoju and tried to present a poem describing his realisation. Shoju received it and crumpled it up in his hand. Through a series of interviews, Hakuin attempted to hang on to his pride, and Shoju, equally vigorously, tried to have him release it, so that his understanding could deepen.

The teacher had to hit the stubborn young monk and even throw him out into a muddy puddle before things could shift. Shoju taunted Hakuin, calling him a 'cave-dwelling Zen corpse'. Eventually Hakuin accepted that there were limits to his understanding and began to practise again in earnest. Shoju gave him something else to ponder: 'When Zen master Nansen was on his deathbed, his students approached and asked, "Where will you be 100 years after your death?"'

One day, while out on a begging round, Hakuin had an even deeper *kensho* than his first one. He hurried back to the hermitage in an ecstasy of joy, and Shoju immediately recognised the young monk's understanding and welcomed him warmly. After staying with Shoju for about eight months, Hakuin continued on with his pilgrimage. He studied with many teachers in many temples. Shoju was, however, the one who rescued him from this spiritual dead-end, and so Hakuin always considered Shoju Rojin his true master.

There's a very good chance that at least some part of your spiritual journey will be unguided. When things get very good, please remember Hakuin. Wonderful experiences are

---

3   Shoju was a hermit and not registered as a temple priest, much less a Zen master. He was only awarded some ranking in the Rinzai school 100 years after his death.

just that – wonderful experiences. If we get attached to them, we trap ourselves.

In his own teaching, Hakuin often refers to a Chinese master called Daiye Soko (1089–1163). I asked Shinzan Rōshi about him. 'Daiye Soko,' he said, '*Koan* Zen, big teacher.' He went on to explain that Daiye was the key person in making *koan* meditation a central part of Zen practice, and spreading it widely throughout Chinese society. If we look into his life and times a little, I think you'll see why *koan* practice is so suitable for our times.

Daiye's China of the 12th century was successful and culturally advanced, but there was a flaw in the system: the most influential and prosperous people found ways to avoid paying their taxes. Over the years the drop in tax revenues led to a gradual weakening in defences.

The decline was so gradual that within the Middle Kingdom this vulnerability was barely noticed. Across the border, however, it was a different matter. In 1127 forces from the Jin state, former allies, poured across the Great Wall. The invaders were well organised and ruthlessly efficient, and, in short order, the northern half of China was occupied and the emperor, with key members of his family, was captured.

China was split and so were the ruling elite, the Mandarins. They found themselves either side of this new contested border. On both sides they faced conflict. In the north the Mandarins' choice was between cooperating with the invaders in the hope of preserving something of Chinese culture, in the knowledge that, should the tides of war turn and the Chinese re-occupy, they would be instantly executed as collaborators. On the other hand, if they resisted the Jin, life was also likely to be dangerous and short.

In the south, the Mandarins had the huge job of trying to recreate the whole political and administrative system of China.

There were splits here too: between those who urged fighting back against the Jin and those who wanted to come to some sort of negotiated settlement.

The Mandarins and those like them – the entire highly educated elite class – were in conditions of terrible stress. They had little time; life was uncertain; they had huge tasks to accomplish. They felt that the fate of Chinese culture was resting on their shoulders. In this predicament, they needed a base of fearlessness and strength to live from, and they needed it fast. Many of them turned to Zen and particularly to the teaching of Daiye Soko. It seems that, in practice, most of these students were lucky to even meet the teacher once or twice. Some communicated by letter; some did just fine by themselves.

I often give students this background sense of where *koan* study comes from because it deals with some misconceptions. People sometimes think they need to be a monk with a teacher on hand to do *koan* study. Actually, as you can see, *koan* study became really popular within a crucible of stress and danger. By comparison, modern life seems idyllic. If the Mandarins did it, why can't you?

Daiye Soko became inadvertently embroiled in the intense political manoeuvrings of his time. He was stripped of his monastic status and exiled to almost certain death in the mosquito-infested south. Undaunted, he continued to help others experience *kensho*.

Despite being fully engaged in teaching, Daiye Soko continued his own development. He is reported to have experienced 18 great enlightenments and countless smaller ones. By the time he died, he left 94 enlightened *dharma* heirs – an unprecedented number.

As a teacher, Daiye Soko was emphatic that all his students should practise the *koan* method of meditation. He was an advocate of sitting meditation, but criticised teachers who over-emphasised it. The times he lived in called for action, and he was a vigorous proponent of meditation and spiritual practice within activity.

A typical teaching would be the following:

> Just steadily go on with your *koan* every moment of your life, whether walking or sitting, so your attention is fixed upon it without interruption. When you begin to find it entirely devoid of flavour, the final moment is approaching. Don't let it slip out of your grasp. Then all of a sudden something flashes in your mind – it will illuminate the entire universe and you will see the spiritual land of the enlightened ones.[4]

At the start of practice, it's normal to feel separate from your *koan*. From this distance you can get a view of it. But gradually you and the *koan* approach one another. Hakuin likes to talk about 'a ball of doubt' or questioning that develops, particularly in the belly. The questioning, the wanting to know, develops a momentum, and your practice allows this momentum to develop, while at the same time maintaining your openness.

In much the same way that in approaching another person you might eventually get close enough to embrace and, when you do, you cannot see them any more, at a certain point you and the *koan* are embraced. Here, as you lose perspective, the *koan* loses meaning.

If you don't pull back, you discover something extraordinary. When you become one with one thing, you become one

---

4   Suzuki, D. (1961) *Essays in Zen Buddhism*, Second Series. New York: Grove Press, p.103.

with everything. A clear-cut, non-dual breakthrough occurs. You find satisfaction and peace.

When you begin *koan* practice, your teacher gives you a particular type of question known as a *hoshin koan*. *Hoshin* (in Japanese) means '*dharma* body', which refers to seeing the enlightened aspect of reality. You experience everything – within and without – as the body of the Buddha. These *hoshin koans* are geared towards giving you a direct perception or direct inroad into unmediated, enlightened reality. 'What is your original face?', 'Does a dog have a Buddha nature?' and 'What is the sound of one hand clapping?' are well-known *hoshin koans*.

Shinzan Rōshi usually gives the *hoshin koan* 'Who are you?' to new practitioners. You'll find some of his *koan* teachings in the section 'Shinzan Rōshi on the *Koan*' in Chapter 13. We'll take this question for our next meditation.

MEDITATION WITH THE KOAN 'WHO AM I?'

As with all these meditation practices, it works well to simply read the instructions slowly and meditatively, and then to put the book down and carry on with your practice. You can find a recorded audio version of these instructions online at www.zenways.org/practical-zen-online (the password is 'insight').

Get comfortable in your sitting place. You can sit on a chair with your feet planted firmly on the floor, you can kneel over a cushion or on a meditation bench, or it may be that you prefer to sit cross-legged on a cushion.

Whichever is most comfortable, you want to create a stable triangular base with your lower body. Make sure your knees are separated and the weight of your upper body is supported by your sitting bones. Sway a little from side to side, forwards and backwards, to find your position of natural uprightness.

Relax your shoulders; have your neck long with the top of your head directly above your sitting bones. Rest your hands in your lap, on a cushion if necessary. Have your mouth closed with your tongue resting gently on the roof. Allow your eyes to lower, or if you wish, you can close them.

Relax your body. Allow your breathing to be natural. Feel the rising and sinking of the breath in your belly.

And now, as you feel settled, relaxed and aware, introduce your *koan*. As you breathe out, ask yourself silently and within, 'Who am I?'

As you breathe in, just allow whatever arises as a result of you posing the question to be seen and known and let go. You may notice thoughts, memories, perceptions, sensations. Let it all come up. Let it all go.

Breathing out: questioning 'Who am I?' Breathing in: allowing.

As you do this, allow all your senses to turn within.

Breath by breath, your body relaxing, your faculties turn to the most important question a human being can ask: Who am I?

Who am I? Keep looking; be curious. Who? Who actually are you?

The two elements of questioning and openness may continue in alignment with the breath, or they may develop another rhythm. Either way is just fine, as long as they both continue.

Breath by breath, build your focus on this question. All kinds of responses, memories and theories might come up. That's fine; let them come.

But there's more to you than any theory. Who are you really? Allow this question to crystallise your focus. With your whole being, examine within.

Over time, the questioning develops a momentum. Zen master Hakuin tells us how this question gradually crystallises into what he calls 'a ball of doubt', or questioning intention. Put this ball down in your belly. Keep looking, sensing deep within.

Breath by breath. Who am I really?

When you discover the answer to this, it won't be any kind of a theory, but an incontrovertible, obvious fact. So continue steadily, turning your senses, your faculties within.

Stay steadily with this practice, with this question. This question is the key to the door of enlightenment. Throw the whole focus of your being into the opening of this door – the doorway to your satisfaction.

Keep questioning. Who? Who? Who am I? Know that you yourself are the answer that you seek. But who are you really? Keep investigating. Who?

In your busy times keep this question in the back of your mind, and in your quiet times bring this question forward. Who are you really?

And as you come to the end of this sitting meditation, gently sway your body side to side. Perhaps stretch a little bit. Slowly come up into standing.

But continue to keep this question with you, knowing that it may be very soon, often sooner than you think, when the whole universe will open up. Your door of enlightenment will open, and you will know directly, clearly, with no shadow of any possible doubt who you really are.

So, in this practice you stay with your *koan*, and you stay with it until there is the clear-cut awakening that Daiye Soko emphasised. There is a pivotal instance of clarity: a 'Before I was blind – Boom! – Now I see' moment. Suddenly you can really understand what those old guys with the strange phrases were talking about!

I once asked Shinzan Rōshi about the way realisation comes in *koan* study as opposed to other kinds of meditation practice. He said, 'Imagine a dirty window – a completely dirty window. No light is coming through. If you want light, what do you do?'

'You clean the window.'

'What are two ways to clean it?'

'Two ways? You could clean it all in broad strokes or you could take a small part of the window and scrub at it until it's clear, and then take another part and so on.'

'Which is faster?'

'I don't know. Maybe the same.'

'No, which is faster to first get the light through?'

'Taking a small part first.'

'This is *koan* study.'

What I took from this is that *koan* study will typically produce a faster initial understanding through its powerful focus. The light coming through is the same, however, whether we work with the breath, the open awareness of the Unborn meditation or with a *koan*.

Daiye Soko often stressed that *koan* study is not an intellectual route. The function of the intellect is to divide and compare. It can't possibly promote the converging process necessary for *koan* study. Daiye Soko was so keen for his students not to take an intellectual scholarly approach that he seized the printing blocks for his teacher's commentary on 100 *koans*, and had them burned. Engo's *Blue Cliff Record* is considered one of Zen's literary masterpieces, so thank goodness copies of the text were saved, but this action by Daiye Soko makes a very powerful point. He also constantly warned against 'dead tree Zen'. Some of the meditation halls at this time were called 'treestump halls' or 'dead tree halls', as the practitioners in them would just sit and sit. Daiye insisted that practice should be a living thing that would bring you alive and give you the power not only to save yourself, but also to serve those around you.

Since Daiye Soko's time, the non-intellectual study of *koans* has become a major thread within Zen. However, over the centuries, local variations in technique have arisen. You might draw on these variations in finding your own way forward with *koan* study.

Korea has an ongoing vigorous Zen tradition that particularly reveres Daiye Soko. In the Korean approach, a Zen master gives a student a question such as the one we heard before: 'What is my original face before my parents were born?' The student stays with that question day after day, month after month, year after year. When an understanding arises, the student goes to the master, who will very often test him or her with other *koans* and questions. However, even if the student demonstrates true understanding and passes the tests, he or she returns there to focus on their original question with the intention of going deeper and deeper with it throughout their whole life.

Within the Chinese tradition, on the other hand, many practitioners chant the Buddha's name as their central practice. The intention is that this chanting leads to the name taking on a life of its own. It continues when you are dreaming, it continues even when you are chatting to friends. Once the chanting is established like this, the student may introduce the question 'Who is calling the Buddha's name?' and, again, this would be the focus of a lifelong study, exploring deeper and deeper who that might be.

So, you can work with one *koan* for the rest of your life and continue to develop. However, within our Japanese tradition, practice has evolved a little differently. As we have learned, Hakuin studied more than one *koan*. This was the approach he advocated. Eventually a system evolved. Two main lineages of *koan* study arose, the Takuju line and the Inzan line, and both use several hundred *koans* arranged in something of a graded syllabus.

The Takuju line has a slightly more intellectual approach and uses a lot of what are known as 'capping' phrases. The student is instructed to look into a *koan* and, when there is an intuitive, direct and immediate understanding, the teacher sends him or her off to look into a special Zen phrasebook composed mostly of lines from some of the greatest Chinese poets. The student has to pick out and present a line of poetry or a phrase that 'caps' or expresses the meaning of the *koan*. Two examples might be the following:

> *Like the sword that cuts but cannot cut itself;*
> *The eye that sees but cannot see itself.*

The cock crows the dawn at dusk;
The sun blazes at midnight.

Over the years the student becomes a living repository of these pithy quotes.

The Inzan line, which Shinzan Rōshi teaches, has a very direct and powerful approach. Master Inzan (1751–1814) as a young monk was given the *koan* 'Put out the fire on the other side of the mountain'. After looking into this phrase, he came to his interview carrying a huge bucket of water and he threw the whole lot over his teacher and all over the walls. The room was wrecked. The Inzan line doesn't use so many of the capping phrases; it emphasises the immediacy and rigour of the student's understanding.

Some people really flourish with the developmental system the *koans* offer. This approach is sometimes called meditation with words, or *kanna-zen*.

Others prefer the silent way, which in Japanese may be called *mokusho-zen*. The Unborn meditation and practice with the breath would be examples of silent practice. Over the years I have found many people on the silent way do very well with one of the *hoshin koans* (the early *koans*), just so they have an initial clear-cut breakthrough.

One of the things about the silent way of practice is that it doesn't tend to have many signposts. Sometimes people doubt they are doing it right or making any progress, and it can feel like they are dithering about for years. Having a clear and definite sense of where the work is heading can be very helpful. But not everyone needs this, and some people do very well with the silent approach all the way. It is down to the individual.

In practical terms everybody needs to be able to enter the deep silence at the heart of everything, and we all need to express our truth within the world. How that manifests with each of us is unique, and I think that is quite how it should be.

There are several questions I am often asked concerning practice with a *koan*, and the first relates to the length of time it takes to work through the 500 or so *koans* in the Japanese system. While we have instances like the Zen master Soen Shaku (1860–1919), who received his master's seal at the age of 24, graduates are usually considerably older. Of course, it is not impossible to see that a devoted monk in a temple full-time with a master on hand may eventually work through all the *koans*, but how on earth can a busy lay individual make significant progress?

There is a theory that it takes 10,000 hours of study to master anything. If you do one hour of meditation a day, you would be looking at around 30 years – a long road by anyone's standard. But if you were to also explore your *koan* in action, as Daiye Soko recommended, and you do this for another hour a day as well, suddenly you are down to 15 years. And if you get a couple of hours a day in like this, you are down to seven years or so.

As mentioned, Daiye Soko worked with people who were at the highest level of government. They were stressed, busy, and trying to keep together a state that was falling apart around them. These men needed a basis to their lives that was meaningful, but they had no time.

Shinzan Rōshi told me that Daiye Soko encouraged his students to utilise the spare attention we all have. Many jobs and chores of daily life such as washing up are mundane and use maybe 30 per cent of our attention. That leaves 70 per cent spare capacity for you to recognise and use well. Daiye Soko's students found they could get something really worthwhile from studying the *koans* while continuing with their regular duties.

So action and the *koan* should be integrated. One of my teachers used to say that *koan* work is a little like being in love. There are times when your loved one is at the forefront of your mind, and other times when he or she is in the background, but the love is nevertheless continuous.

For the *koan* process, the more you can move towards this continuity of questioning, the more rapidly the process tends to go. Zen uses lots of images to explain this, such as the creation of fire with fire sticks. If you do a little bit of rubbing, put them down and then try again, you'll be there trying to get the fire started for evermore, but if you keep a constant rhythm, the spark comes quickly.

It's also important to stress that *koan* study isn't a piecemeal business. Typically you'll be working with a *koan* for some time without feeling as though you are making progress. Then suddenly, and often unexpectedly, you will experience a breakthrough, and in the aftermath quickly pass a series of other *koans*.

It is worth mentioning here that, although a teacher is not essential when working with a *koan*, he or she will most likely save you time. If you find someone who has at least walked the course before you, they can help you see if you're doing it right or if you're intellectualising.

It's also easy to become side-tracked or just bored, and sometimes this practice can be somewhat threatening too. In a sense you are loosening your grip on life, and this can make you feel temporarily unsettled. A teacher may help you find another perspective in which you notice that all your daily functions, such as getting dressed, eating and going to work, all continue. And this rootless feeling doesn't last forever.

This brings us to the second common question, which is whether *koan* study is safe without a teacher on hand. Back in the days when teachers such as Daiye Soko were working, only a tiny minority of lay students were able to see their teacher regularly. Some could correspond with their teacher (and, in fact, Daiye Soko's letters are regarded as one of the great masterpieces of Zen literature), but that was about it.

These days we have convenient and cheap ways of communicating across great distances, and it is possible to have an active and ongoing relationship with a teacher on the other side of the world. I have students in China, Japan, Spain, the USA and many other places, and they do absolutely fine.

I occasionally meet people who, like Hakuin, have gone off completely by themselves to do *koan* practice. They have often done very well too.

The third question that frequently arises is that previously we emphasised bringing mindfulness or presence to whatever we're doing, and now it seems that, with *koan* practice, we're splitting the attention.

Actually, this is not correct. One of the reasons Shinzan Rōshi likes to begin with the question 'Who are you?' is because it can so easily be transferred into action. For example, when we are weeding, the *koan* becomes 'Who is weeding?', when we are making dinner, 'Who is chopping these carrots?', and so on. With subsequent *koan* study, we learn how to hold the *koan* close while we act – in the way that a pregnant mother holds her growing baby close.

Right now I recommend you spend one week practising with the 'Who am I?' *koan* for 25 minutes followed by five minutes writing in your meditation diary. This will give you the chance to become familiar with the process. As for deeper insights? Hakuin liked to talk about a student who found the way in two days. For most of us, it's a rather more prolonged process.

In the next chapter we're going to look at keeping you healthy and strong along the way.

CHAPTER 5

FROM SICKNESS TO HEALTH

Soft Ointment Meditation

What is the use of finding enlightenment if the process of getting there leaves you too weak to live out its truth? And if you start out frazzled and ungrounded, what kind of results are you likely to get?

Genuine spiritual work can be tough, and many faiths recognise the demands made on their people. From the Christian perspective, Saint John of the Cross wrote of spiritual proficients, those with contemplative experience, as 'subject therein to great infirmities and sufferings and physical derangements, and consequently weariness of mind'.[1]

Zen is by no way excluded from these demands. I have experienced practising in a Zen monastery that did not emphasise the work we are now going to cover. It seemed that the longer people practised, the sicker they got. At one time five out of the six most senior people were suffering from serious energy depletion conditions such as ME (myalgic encephalitis) and fibromyalgia.

---

1   Saint John of the Cross (1934) *The Mystical Doctrine*. Selected by R.H.J. Stewart. London: Sheed and Ward, p.92.

How would it be to practise in a way that boosts your health, rather than undermines it? Hakuin grappled with this problem for some years, and here we are going to look at his life to learn how he dealt with severe sickness, and how he came to restore his health.

This work is particularly relevant, not to say vital, for us living in this sensory-saturated, media-dominated, disembodied, heady age.

One of my students in London commented to me:

'These days physical work is dying out. Many of us spend long hours looking at screens, both at work and in leisure time. Those of us in the city are constantly bombarded with sensory stimulation. When I look back, it's no wonder I got so frazzled.'

In addition, much of what passes for spiritual work and meditation even further emphasises this heady quality.

There is no sign of any of these forces diminishing. Combined, they encourage us to live in a disconnected, weakening and out-of-body way.

Let's consider how things could be. Take a moment to imagine feeling washed clean inside as well as out, your upper body light and open, your lower body empowered and strong. Close your eyes and feel into this. Try to stay here for a full minute.

This is our direction.

For much of his early life, Hakuin meditated intensively with *koans*. Initially his whole-hearted practice worked well. He had numerous powerful realisations of *kensho*, or spiritual breakthrough, and was thus able to spend his later life helping others to wake up. But there were consequences. After a few years of this intensity, Hakuin's health began to suffer.

Gradually his symptoms worsened. Describing them he wrote:

> My heart overheated and scorched my lungs. My legs felt as cold as icy snow. I constantly heard noises in my ears as if I was walking along through a river valley. My liver felt weak; I was afraid of everything. My spirit was distressed and weary. Whether sleeping or awake, I saw illusions and visions. My armpits were constantly drenched with sweat and my eyes continually filled with tears.[2]

Feeling progressively weaker, Hakuin needed help. He visited doctors and Zen masters. He struggled to find anyone who didn't just throw up their hands. Eventually, as he writes in his account, *Yasenkana* (translated in Chapter 13), he heard of a hermit living in Shirakawa, in the mountains north east of Kyoto, and he set out to seek him. Hakuin describes wandering through the mountains, eventually finding the hermit, Hakuyushi, living in a cave. At first Hakuyushi tried to turn the young man away, claiming to be just an ignorant old fool. But Hakuin refused to be put off, and he persuaded the hermit to examine him.

---

2 Ekaku, H. *Yasenkana*; see the section '*Yasenkana (Night Boat Conversation)* by Hakuin Zenji' in Chapter 13 for the source of this quotation.

Underlying Hakuyushi's diagnosis was the viewpoint of the human organism as an energetic phenomenon. The hermit was able to describe exactly how Hakuin had unbalanced himself by unbalancing his bodily energies and, more importantly, gave him a series of meditative practices to restore his health.

Over the following three years Hakuin put the hermit's practices into action and restored his health completely. The transformation was remarkable. In his twenties Hakuin was weak and sickly, even contemplating the approach of death. After his recovery he was noted for great power and vitality, even well into his eighties.

How is this relevant for us? Well, for a number of reasons. Let's define some terms. In my Zen training I was taught to characterise people into three groups. The first group we can call the 'gutsy' types. Their centre is based in the abdomen (called *hara* in Japanese). As the name indicates, these people have a courageous, energised, grounded and intuitive approach to life. The second group are the 'hearty' types. Their centre is based in the heart area. They are typically ruled by their emotions. Whatever is the dominant feeling of the moment is the major driving force in their lives. The third group are the 'heady' types. There are three main heady categories: the overly intellectual types; those who are over-sensitive (the senses are primarily located in the head); and those who have opened up spiritually without fully knowing what they're doing.

As mentioned, these days many, many of us are heady types.

In the West we tend not to love our bellies. Our view of abdominal cultivation frequently amounts to endless punishing sit-ups with the overall intention of making the belly disappear. It's absolutely fine to be slim, of course, but simply armouring this part of the body with a muscular corset misses so much of what the belly can be. In East Asian spiritual culture it is a given that we can cultivate the belly and develop this 'gutsy' attitude to life. As it builds, we take on a gravitas and charisma, as well as an elevated level of energy. This is an important reason why people go to Zen temples to prepare for future success in life.

Hakuin's Zen teaching combined what he learned from his two primary teachers. He took the thoroughgoing investigation of the truth of things emphasised by Shoju Rojin (*rikan*, or 'contemplation of reality') and combined it with the *naikan* ('inner contemplation') he learned from Hakuyushi. He taught, 'They are what two wings are to a bird; what two wheels are to a cart.'[3]

Initially, however, Hakuin laid aside his *rikan* work for three years so he could fully integrate the *naikan* practices and restore his health. Let's follow his lead and concentrate for now on the *naikan*. This first of these practices we're going to explore is called *nanso no ho* – the 'soft ointment' or 'soft milk' meditation.

SOFT OINTMENT MEDITATION

Read over these instructions slowly and then practise at your own pace. You can find a recorded audio version of these instructions online at www.zenways.org/practical-zen-online (the password is 'insight').

Practise for 25 minutes. First, get comfortable in your sitting place – on a chair, kneeling over a cushion or meditation bench, or cross-legged on a cushion.

---

3 Yampolsky, P.B. (editor and translator) (1971) *The Zen Master Hakuin*. Oretegama I. New York: Columbia University Press, p.50.

Create a stable triangular base with your lower body by separating your knees. Sway a little from side to side to find your position of relaxed uprightness. Release your shoulders; have your neck long with the top of your head directly above your sitting bones. Rest your hands in your lap and soften your tongue, letting it rest broadly on the roof of your mouth. Soften and lower your eyes; if you wish you can keep them softly open, or if you prefer, you can close them fully. Allow your breathing to be natural, and tune into the movement of your breath in the belly.

Bring your awareness to the top of your head and imagine how it would be if you had a large, soft ball the size of a duck egg, made up of fragrant, healing ointment or milk just resting there. How would this feel? This ointment has a special property in that not only does it melt and run down over your body, it also melts through to bathe inside your body.

The heat of your head causes this egg to begin to melt. The soothing liquid begins to flow, down, down, over your head. And inside your head too, sinking and flowing and cleansing as it pours downwards.

Passing over the little muscles around your eyes, feel it soaking into your temples and over the back of your head. Feel it flowing in your neck, releasing and relaxing. It enters your jaw muscles, and as it passes through it cools and soothes, all the while healing and softening.

And now the ointment melts down through your neck, down your throat and into your shoulders, healing, soothing and flowing, causing all the tensions and twists, all the tightness and knots, to release and soften.

As it reaches the top of your chest, the ointment continues to glide down, inside and around your lungs and heart, calming and healing. It flows, cooling and loosening down through your arms, down over your arms to your fingertips.

From your head more and more of this milk flows down through your brain, gently dissolving and releasing all the tension and struggles, gently allowing you to let go. And as before, it flows down and down over your face, down your neck and throat, and into your chest. Relaxing and resting, releasing your heart and lungs, freeing you to just be.

Feel the ointment flowing down through the centre of your body, down your back, down through every vertebrae, releasing and resting. Notice it melting and releasing around and through your lower organs, always softening.

And more and more flows down. Over your face, down and down into your belly, deeper and deeper, taking all the tension and all the fight. Allowing calming softness, it flows down and around and in, soaking, through your pelvis, releasing and soothing.

Still even more releases over your head, fragrant and soothing; your ointment soaks down through your pelvis and slowly soaks through your legs, knees and down.

And now it is melting down through your arms, your wrists, your hands. Soaking and gliding down into your ankles, deeper and deeper, pouring and flowing all through every part of you, healing and melting. This soothing ointment, pouring and flowing down through your feet, soaks in and around your toes so that your whole body is washed. Washed and softened and healed.

Now imagine that this flow, which has gone down all the way to your feet, begins to accumulate, to fill your legs, your pelvis and your abdomen all the way to the level of your navel.

So now your upper body can feel washed clean and clear, and your lower body is filled, energised, strong.

Take a little time to rest in this feeling. And now have a stretch. Allow your eyes to open. Do your best to stay in this place, even as you go about your normal business.

If you practise like this, every day, for 25 minutes over a week, you'll soon not need the guidance and can fully make the method your own. It won't take long before your whole system will re-orientate in the way Zen master Hakuin describes. This pleasurable practice really works.

You may be one of those people who wonder about this rather archetypal meeting with the hermit in the mountains. You wouldn't be the first. Over the years there has been considerable debate about the existence of Hakuyushi and Hakuin's claims to have practised with him.

In Hakuin's accounts of his meetings with the hermit, and we have several, there are statements such as the following: 'There were rumours that he was 300 years old.' It's no surprise these outlandish claims caused some students of Zen to wonder whether the man was Hakuin's invention. Certainly Hakuin loved a good story!

These suspicions have prompted quite a bit of research over the years. The first investigator, Torei, was Hakuin's student and main successor. Torei travelled to Shirakawa himself to see what he could discover. He came across a rock-cutter working in a quarry. This man told Torei that his father had introduced the hermit to his cave, so Torei came away believing Hakuyushi had indeed existed. In addition to this evidence, other well-known writers recorded their meetings with the hermit.

The controversy was settled, however, in more recent times. In the 1960s a researcher called Ito Kazuo found a death record in Jogan-in, a temple in Shirakawa. The note records that the hermit 'fell from a cliff on the 23rd day of the seventh month, 1709, and died two days later on the 25th. He had lived in the mountains for forty-eight years...'[4] In May 2013 I hiked into the mountains above Shirakawa and was able to find the remains of the cave, together with the memorial stone. All around, you can still see evidence of the quarrying from ages past.

We still have a problem, however. The hermit died the year before Hakuin claims to have met him. It is possible that Hakuin got mixed up with his dates, as he wrote all this down 30 years after the event. Perhaps he met Hakuyushi just before he died. We'll never know for sure. Whether Hakuin studied with the hermit as he describes, or simply used him as a literary device to get across teachings he learned elsewhere, the fact remains that he strongly emphasised these methods of vitality cultivation in his teaching.

The most well-known account of these methods is in his book, *Yasenkana* (see the translation in Chapter 13). Describing his sickness and his meeting with Hakuyushi the hermit, the book is a manual on restoring health, and building wellbeing and vitality. In the two-and-a-half centuries since its first publication, *Yasenkana* has not only been successfully used

---

4   Waddell, N. (editor and translator) (2009) *Hakuin's Precious Mirror Cave.* Berkeley, CA: Counterpoint, p.86.

by Zen monks, but also by martial artists and many of the general population seeking better health.

As mentioned, Hakuin describes how for three years he laid his regular Zen practice aside and put the hermit's teachings into practice. This undoubtedly led to his recovery, but it was his subsequent spiritual journey that allowed him to develop the fully integrated practice he went on to teach his students.

After his health was restored, the next significant stage in his life found Hakuin on a mountain called Iwatakisan in central Japan. This is just a few miles from Gyokuryuji, the temple where I practised. Here, Hakuin retired for almost two years of solitary retreat. Up on the mountain, practising intensely, he experienced a series of spiritual openings so powerful that he would dance with joy. Eventually he reached a condition of complete fearlessness that stayed with him throughout his whole life.

Meanwhile, word came that all was not well back in his home village. His father had become very sick and the village temple, Shoinji, was now unoccupied and falling down. Hakuin returned home, took up residence in the temple, and attended his ailing father. Even though the temple was in a terrible condition and sited in the centre of a bustling village, Hakuin carried on a version of the retreat schedule he had followed when he was up on the mountain. He describes in his autobiography how every night he would adopt the *zazen* position, then instruct one of the temple boys to wrap a futon around him and tie it on with a rope to keep him in an upright position. He would sit tied up in meditation right through to morning.

It seems that it was during this time that Hakuin worked out a way to combine the teachings of Hakuyushi with his Zen *koan* study. Gradually word got out about the earnest and deeply realised monk in the tiny temple, and students started to appear – not only the local villagers who began to enquire about Zen, but also male and female monastics from further afield. Hakuin began to teach, somewhat reluctantly, as he felt his own practice wasn't yet complete.

And then one night, in 1726, when he was 41 years old and had been resident at Shoinji for a decade, he sat studying the *Lotus Sutra*, perhaps the most venerated Buddhist text in Japan. A cricket started to shrill in the foundations of the temple and, as he heard this noise, the whole universe opened up for him. He let out an involuntary shout and began to weep. From this time on Hakuin lived in a state of complete liberation, and for the next 40 years he devoted himself to his students. This teaching effort included *sanzen* (one-to-one interviews), as well as lecturing to increasingly large groups. He also wrote many books on Zen.

Before long the tiny temple was filled with Zen students. Hakuin didn't move to larger premises; instead, he began to gather the overflowing monks into groups of three, and sent them off into the surrounding countryside. These monks would live in old shrines, fishermen's huts, under trees – anywhere they could find shelter. Eventually it reached a point where the whole landscape was a kind of monastery without walls.

We have an account from a famous poet, Takatsuki Rikei, who came to visit Hakuin in 1753. Rikei describes how there were about 150 monastic students, of whom ten lived in the temple. The other 140 would come in at different times during the day for their *sanzen* and then return to their dwellings. This grassroots, spontaneous *dharma* centre was unique. Nothing quite like it has happened since.

You can imagine the austere living conditions of these monks. Maintaining their health so that they could continue with their practice became a priority, and Hakuin taught them what he had learned from Hakuyushi, about preserving health, energy and strength. From these improvised, homespun conditions, Hakuin produced a great number of enlightened students who were grounded in the ways of building energy and power. Over succeeding generations these students spread throughout Japan. A modern commentator writes:

> The dynamism demonstrated by Hakuin and his disciples in their 'takeover' of most Japanese Rinzai monasteries within a few decades presumably is not unrelated to the insistence they placed on breathing and vital energy, and their rejection of the use of *koans* as a literary exercise.[5]

All Rinzai practitioners in Japan are now of Hakuin's lineage, and all other lineages of Rinzai Zen have died out. Every contemporary Japanese Rinzai teacher looks back to Hakuin as an ancestor.

From personal experience, I have found the hermit's teachings to be tremendously valuable, both in surviving a tough temple schedule on little sleep, and in handling life in the big city. Compared with Zen students of the past, of course, our living conditions are incredibly luxurious, but the spiritual challenges remain the same. In addition we have other pressures on us. Perhaps chief of these is our bombardment by sensory stimulation.

One of my London Zen students described the differences he found when working with the *naikan* practices:

---

5   Mohr, M. (2000) 'Emerging from Nonduality: Koan Practice in the Rinzai Tradition Since Hakuin.' In S. Heine and D. Wright (2000) *The Koan: Texts and Contexts in Zen Buddhism*. Oxford: Oxford University Press, p.266.

'I have a tough job. I'm on the phone half the day trying to make sales. I have a pile of other things to do. There's never enough time. On top of that I have to practically fight my way into work, and it used to be that by the time I got home I was exhausted. If I tried to meditate I'd simply start nodding off. Since I've been doing these practices, I've got more oomph. I can handle the commute with more grace. I can get through work. And in the evenings and weekends I can actually do some useful meditation practice. The difference is remarkable.'

Take a week to explore this soft ointment meditation, and then we'll add the next piece of the puzzle.

CHAPTER 6

CULTIVATING GUTS

Energising Your Hara

> Bring your mind to your fingertips for a moment. It's very easy to do: simply shift your attention here. Notice what you can feel. Now do the same thing, but this time your destination is the abdomen. Bring your mind to your belly by settling your attention here. Although you may feel less than you do in your fingertips, just notice what you can sense. Rest like this for a few moments.

Very likely you won't experience much, at least initially, when you shift your attention like this. With persistence, however, the belly comes alive and we feel empowered and grounded. But in the early stages it's a subtle business. This waking up the belly is nevertheless a key element in our work. We're going to explore a simple way to accelerate and clarify this process.

One time at Gyokuryuji we had a visit from a sword master. It was autumn and the deciduous trees in the garden were gleaming golden and red. In front of the main hall he set up a stand holding an upright roll of tatami straw matting, which had the approximate dimensions of a human figure.

He stood in front of the roll, traditionally dressed, with his sword sheathed by his side. He seemed to be going through some sort of inner procedure of strong breathing. Then he began to move. His movements had the deliberate power of an awakening snake. He slowly drew the sword. The blade leapt into life, flashed left and right, slicing the matting into tumbling segments. His movement slowed again as he sheathed the sword and entered stillness.

'Learn from him,' Shinzan Rōshi said to me.

I had no great interest in becoming a swordsman, and the master's visit was a short one. Nevertheless, I approached him and we began to talk. He emphasised many points we've already covered: the *hara*, and in particular, the spot a little below the navel in the centre of the body called the *tanden*. He then taught me a breathing method to activate the abdomen and make it your centre of gravity. It's fast. The whole thing takes just nine breaths. I've never come across anything that gives such a clear sense of being grounded in the *hara* so quickly, so I want to share it with you.[1]

First, where are we going with this? Hakuin describes an energised and activated *hara* thus: '...the space below your navel will swell like a gourd and soon becomes full like an inflated leather ball.'[2] In my experience this work doesn't have to lead to a protrusion of the belly, more a sense of inner strength or resilience, or what these days we would call 'intra-abdominal pressure'.

Underlying Zen, in common with many aspects of traditional East Asian culture, is a sense that the human

---

1 I don't know this teacher's sword tradition. My friend John Maki Evans, one of the most highly qualified Japanese sword practitioners in the world, has encountered similar practices, but not exactly this one.

2 Ekaku, H. *Yasenkana*; see the section '*Night Boat Conversation* by Hakuin Zenji' in Chapter 13 for the source of this quotation.

system is underpinned by vitality. Called *ki* (or in Chinese, *qi* or *chi*), this vitality can be depleted by certain activities and augmented by others. Someone with depleted *ki* is more likely to become ill, and someone with plenty of *ki* will tend to be vigorous and strong. This *ki* is seen to run along certain routes in the body, and these routes have connections with certain physical organs, emotions and mind states.

Of course, all of this is completely discounted by the modern Western medical model. In practice you don't have to believe in energy or even feel energy to get the benefits of the practices we're exploring in this book. Regardless of what you believe or don't believe, if you do the work, you'll get the effects.

So how is it to be grounded in the *hara*? A famous teacher of *hara* cultivation, Okada Torajiro, wrote, 'Those who regard the belly as the most important part, and who have built the stronghold where the spirit can grow – these are the people of the highest rank. Strength flows out from them and produces a spiritual condition of ease and equanimity.'[3]

Cultivating the *hara* is not a complicated business. Underlying the method we'll be exploring is a principle that energy follows intention, and intention is primarily marked by attention. When you put your mind in the belly, your energy follows. So intention guides this process. We're going to incorporate breath and sound to provide a vehicle for this intention. As you get used to the process, you'll need the breath and sound less and less: intention alone will do the work for you.

I was taught using the sounds 'ah' and 'un'. These are the first and last sounds of the Japanese language system.

---

3   Quoted in Dürckheim, K.G. (2004) *Hara, the Vital Center of Man*. Rochester, VT: Inner Traditions.

'Ah', the first sound in the Japanese syllabary, is seen as the sound you make at birth. 'Un', the syllable that comes last, is also your final sound. 'Ah' is the inhalation that begins life, 'un' the exhalation of release. So the whole of life is contained in these two sounds coupled with their respective parts of the breath – thus the in-breath and out-breath can both serve in energising the abdomen.

When you approach a fully laid-out temple, the entrance gate is usually guarded by a pair of muscled giants called *nio*. The first is named Agyo. He has his mouth open to represent the inhalation that begins life – the 'ah' in-breath in this practice. The other, called Ungyo, has his mouth closed and represents the 'un' out-breath.

As well as the in-breath and out-breath, there is a third element. To understand the importance of this, you need to know that energy can accumulate in different places. The belly is seen as being your battery pack. Tradition says that energy can accumulate there and safely distribute throughout your entire system. Your chest area is different. Energy building there can overheat the heart and become extremely uncomfortable, painful even. Similarly in your head, excess energy can cause headaches and mental disturbances. Our third element enhances the energy movement into the belly and also has a safety function. After the 'ah' sound, we swallow a little saliva and imagine we're swallowing it down to the belly. When you're doing this right, it carries the energy down, the chest sinks and softens, and the belly strengthens.

We're going to divide the abdominal area into three zones – front, sides and back. I suggest you read through the instructions below first, and then start to follow along. Don't worry if it seems to take a little time to get it right.

BUILDING YOUR *HARA*

Now that we have looked at the benefits of bringing the intention to the belly, we are going to learn to really ground in this place. This practice will help keep you vital, powerful and grounded in the world. I recommend starting with the standing position, but if you need to sit or lie for any reason, this works just fine.

Although this is quite a strong breathing exercise, it is important to note that the breath is used as a vehicle for your intention. It is your intention that's key. So, if you have medical problems that make this kind of strong breathing problematic, simply breathe lightly and use your intention alone to get the same result. If in doubt, take it very gently. Read through the instructions once or twice before putting them into practice. As with all the other practices, you can find a recorded audio version of these instructions online at www.zenways. org/practical-zen-online (the password is 'insight').

Stand with your feet hip-width apart. Make sure your knees are soft and your pelvis is aligned. You don't want your tail sticking out or particularly tucked under – just establish it as evenly as you can.

The 'ah' sound goes with the in-breath, and the 'un' sound with the out-breath. To begin with, let's practise making the sounds.

In the English language we don't normally make sounds using the in-breath. Many languages do this, however, and you may have done it yourself, for example while playing as a child. Just to familiarise yourself, say 'Good morning, how are you?' on an in-breath. It's not particularly hard to do. Say it a couple of times if it helps you get more comfortable with doing this. If this seems difficult, imagine you've just been shocked and take a rapid breath in – 'ahhh!' You'll make the correct sound almost automatically.

Now, to make the 'ah' sound in the practice, open your mouth. As the air flows in, create a light resistance in the back of your throat, to produce a fairly high-pitched sound. It doesn't have to be loud. Take the air in as deep as you can, but do your best not to lift your chest. The air comes into your belly, which swells as your diaphragm falls.

Practise the 'ah' sound over five breaths, breathing in with the 'ah' sound, breathing out normally.

Now let's examine the 'un' sound. This is on the exhalation. Close your mouth, and as you breathe out through your nose, make a deep 'unnn' sound, like a contented, purring lion. Feel the pressure building in your belly as you breathe all the way out.

Familiarise yourself with the 'un' sound over five breaths with a silent in-breath.

Now you are going to use this breathing to energise the *hara*. As mentioned, the breath is used not just for the belly, but also the sides and back, so the whole area beneath the ribcage is involved.

Let's just build some connection with our areas of focus. Do a few gentle breaths into the belly. Allow the area to soften and release. Have your hands resting on your belly and let them move in and out.

Move your hands around to the sides of your belly (your waist), and see if they move in and out with your breathing. Try to notice them rising and sinking.

Now move your hands to your back and let them swell and release, as you gently breathe. At first it may seem a little harder to feel some movement. Don't worry, just do your best and see what you notice.

Now return your attention to the front of your belly. Place your hands here. Take an 'ah' breath in. At the peak of the 'ah', before you begin exhaling, take a little saliva and swallow. Let the energy and any tension in your head or chest drop into your belly. As you do this, lift your perineum (pelvic floor). Exhale through your nose with a deep, long 'un'. Feel the energy enter your belly. Feel your belly pressure increase beneath your hands. Release in your pelvic floor. Repeat this strong breathing three times, keeping your attention in the belly and remembering to swallow a little saliva between each 'ah' inhalation and 'un' exhalation.

Now move your attention to your sides. Repeat the breathing three times, keeping your awareness on the rising and sinking in your sides.

And now move your awareness to the back of your *hara*, your lower back. It often helps to lean forward just a little and place your hands on your back. Take an 'ah' in-breath. Try to feel your back swell beneath your hands. Swallow, and this time, as you exhale, make the 'un' sound with your attention in your back. Repeat this twice more.

Now relax your breathing and just stand, paying attention to any sensations you may feel, particularly in your *hara*. I recommend finishing off with a few minutes of slow walking meditation, gently resting your attention on your breath to allow everything to settle and integrate.

Let the whole process take 25 minutes. Then take five minutes to write in your meditation diary.

This breathing may feel a little strange to begin with, but most people quite quickly get the hang of it. Just gently persist, doing the nine breaths once a day for a week. You'll begin to develop more of a sense of what it means to energise the *hara*. You may find you generate a warmth in the area below your ribs and a kind of broad, grounded feeling. Take it gently.

Let's look a bit more at this *hara* cultivation.

Traditionally, here in the West, we have thought of the mind and body as separate. In more recent times this dichotomy has been found to be a gross oversimplification. Your nervous system is distributed throughout your body. Body and mind are actually one, and so, not surprisingly, what we call 'a gut feeling' really does have a basis in your physiology.

As you know, in Zen we meditate with *koans*, questions that cannot be solved with the intellect. In fact, the more you try to intellectualise, the more frustrated you become. There is a purpose here. It is not that the intellectual mind is a bad thing or a problem, but rather, it can be compared to a computer or processor. It isn't equipped to run your life; it is simply not the right tool for that job. Your intellect divides and compares. It doesn't find underlying unity.

It would be like the prime minister of a country allowing a think-tank of advisers to run the country. The think-tank is great at coming up with good ideas, new possibilities and a wide range of perspectives on things, but it is not the leader. It cannot run the show. If it attempts the job, it comes under terrible stress and is less able to perform the functions it was once good at.

So when you work with a *koan* that cannot be answered intellectually, you learn to activate another mode of knowing, another mode of processing. One of the characteristics of this other mode of knowing is that it is non-dual. Sometimes Zen calls it *not-knowing*.

We have discussed the duality of our adult consciousness already, and you can see evidence of this way of thinking everywhere. Our language, arts, research and whole worldviews are based on the perception that 'this is me; that is the universe'. Life experiences build on each other to entrench this view. Intrinsic to this worldview is the sense that I am insignificant and vulnerable in this hostile universe, and sooner or later I will be destroyed. Life is a battle for existence. And from this viewpoint, life is inevitably a tragedy. It's simply a game we cannot win.

But this dualistic worldview is actually just that – only a view. There is a whole other way of knowing who you are and how you exist, and this other way is based on intuitive knowing. It is a place beyond dualities. Within this place you can know for yourself, without any shadow of a doubt, that you are not separate.

On this level you were not born and you cannot die. You are absolutely indestructible and there is nothing to fear. Far from being a tragedy, life is an absolutely exquisite unfolding of this beautiful unity. You can live within this knowing. And you can bring this knowing into flower through meditation practice. An important aspect of this flowering is allowing your guts their place.

There is a relatively new branch of science called 'neuro-gastroenterology', which explores the enteric nervous system (ENS) or 'the brain in the gut'. As an embryo grows, the brain, nervous system and the ENS all develop from one clump of tissue called the 'neural crest'. The ENS nerve cells are found in the tissue lining your oesophagus, stomach, intestines and colon. Researcher Dr Michael Gershon says this 'brain-like' system has more than 100 million nerve cells in the small intestine alone: roughly equal to the number of nerve cells in the spinal cord.

This gut-brain is also a comprehensive chemical warehouse containing every one of the classes of neurotransmitter found in the brain. As a 'second brain', it can send and receive neurochemical impulses, respond to emotions and record experiences to be stored as memory. All these complex neural and neurochemical connections make it possible for us to have what we call 'gut feelings'.

In contrast to the head-brain, the kind of knowing of the gut-brain, or *hara*, is all-embracing. As we develop the *hara*, we bring about groundedness and steadiness, but we also develop this intuitive knowing. And in addition we have a far more energised life. It is good for our health and wellbeing, as well as for our spiritual unfolding.

The *hara* also has an important role in dealing with negative emotions. We tend to deal with such emotions in two ways. We may try to pretend they don't exist by suppressing them. Alternatively, we may act out the emotion in one way or another. Neither way is helpful or healthy. We need a third way.

A very powerful method we have already mentioned is to simply provide a space for these negative emotions to come and go during your meditation time. The *hara* is such a space. Here feelings can come and go. They are not squashed, nor allowed to cause havoc; they are simply observed and accepted.

Suppose you were in a room with a very frightened puppy. If you tried to chase it around to grab and control it, you would only make it more frightened. If you were to walk out of the room and slam the door, it would become more agitated. But if you sit down quietly in the room and do nothing, the puppy will gradually settle, and come and make friends with you. Its fear will melt away. We can do the same thing with negative aspects of ourselves. When you encounter fear or anger or any other aspect of yourself that causes you pain, simply give it space. Allow the feelings to be loved without pushing them away or running from them. This space, or presence, is what compassion really is. Negative emotions will heal wherever compassion is present. The *hara*, as it develops and becomes a conscious part of your being, is an arena where this healing can happen.

CHAPTER 7

STANDING STRONG

Including Your Legs

'Have the face of a Buddha and the legs of a donkey,' said Zen master Dogen.[1]

> Just for a moment close your eyes. Become aware of your toes, your feet, your ankles, your legs, your hips and your pelvis up to the level of your navel. Spend five breaths resting your attention in this area. Notice how you feel. Now open your eyes. Perhaps you can maintain this feeling as you read on.

There is a principle in Zen that the higher you rise, the more important it is to have a strong grounding. Zen master Daishin, my first Zen teacher, often spoke of the lotus blossom that must keep its roots planted in the mud or else die. It is in the mud of our everyday life that we find our nourishment. It is also

---

1   A paraphrase from Leighton, T.D. and Okamura, S. (1996) *Dogen's Pure Standards for the Zen Community: A Translation of the Eihei Shingi.* New York: SUNY Press.

in the mud we have our arena of expression: the living truth of Zen. Insight that has not yet found its way into concrete expression is immature.

Zen master Hakuin wrote, 'Of what use is it to awaken to the essential points of the Five Houses and Seven Schools (of Zen)[2] and then to die young?'[3] Perceiving your true nature, the experience of enlightenment, is not the end of practice, but the beginning. It is the expression of your true nature throughout your life that will enable you to truly make a difference in the world for your own benefit and for the benefit of others.

In certain religions and spiritual cultures, dying young after finding your spiritual basis wouldn't matter at all, and might even be a cause for celebration. For example, many of the spiritual practices imported directly from India were developed for the use of spiritual mendicants – those who leave behind their families and devote themselves full-time to a spiritual life. In the eyes of that society such people are considered already dead, so there is little need for much concern over the physical effects of their practices.

The cultures of East Asia, China, Japan and Korea take a very different viewpoint. There is an emphasis on longevity, and those who live a long and healthy life are considered worthy of respect. We are here for a reason and we have work to do. Development of the spiritual dimension, it is believed, should never undermine the body's integrity. Ageing, sickness and death are inevitable, but we can make the choice to live well.

---

2 The Five Houses of Zen refer to the Rinzai, Soto, Igyo, Ummon and Hogen lineages (all but the first two have now died out). The Seven Schools of Zen refer to seven of the branches of Rinzai lineage.

3 Yampolsky, P.B. (editor and translator) (1971) *The Zen Master Hakuin*. Oretegama I. New York: Columbia University Press, p.51.

Another way of thinking about contrasting spiritual cultures is to divide them into 'body-positive' and 'body-negative' mindsets. In the West, under the influence of Plato, a body-negative view largely prevailed. Here a person is seen as being composed of two distinct and separate parts: the inferior, animalistic body that imprisons the superior soul. Life is characterised as a struggle with the spirit seeking release from our animal nature. The world, in this mindset, is typically seen as a place of trial and testing, and our real home lies elsewhere.

In Zen there is generally a more holistic body-positive approach, well described by Soyen Shaku, the first Zen master to teach in America:

> For convenience sake, I take the mind as the subjective aspect of the body, and the body as the objective aspect of the mind. To speak more popularly, the mind is the inner side of the body and the body is the outer case of the mind. They both make up one solid reality.[4]

When we consider this whole-being mindset, it obviously makes sense that we should foster and indeed celebrate our connection to the earth.

Zen master Jinshu (630–706) began a teaching poem:

> *The body is a wisdom tree;*
> *The mind a bright mirror.*[5]

---

4   Shaku, S. (2003) *Zen for Americans*. Whitefish, MT: Kessinger Publishing Co., p.96.
5   Author's translation, based on http://en.wikipedia.org/wiki/Huineng

The second line might remind you of the teachings of Zen master Bankei. The first gives us a wonderful image for the body-positive way. It is essential to develop roots for this tree. From the roots the spiritual tree can grow tall and strong.

The physical power of a strong root was demonstrated to me in Japan by one of our temple practitioners, Aikido master Shuji Ozeki Sensei. This man, who founded the Aikikai branch of Aikido in Australia, delighted in pitting his tiny frame against bigger and stronger opponents. Not only did he gleefully use the energy of their aggression against them, he could also make himself immobile, as if he was glued to the ground.

Ozeki Sensei and Shinzan Rōshi had been fellow students at Shogenji, which was known as the strictest Zen training monastery in Japan. They had both studied with Itsugai Kajiura Rōshi, a teacher with a fearsome reputation, and in the vigorous and forceful training, both men were required to develop a powerful connection to the earth.

By contrast, I remember meeting one new-age spiritual teacher in Glastonbury, England. It was rumoured that this man could read his students' minds with ease, but despite this ability he was permanently sickly. He hated the cold British weather, and his skinny frame caused him great suffering, particularly in winter. His whole being was focused upwards; he seemed to have a huge head on tiny shoulders.

Very few of us are as spiritually open and elevated as this man, but even so you may find yourself 'uptight'. Stress, tension, physical inactivity and the intensely stimulating culture we live in combine to draw us up and out of ourselves. We become ungrounded and lose our root, and this makes us weak.

Have you spent a day in a busy city and found yourself completely frazzled? It doesn't have to be this way. When our centre or root is strong, we can actually gain strength from this stimulation. It is only when our root is weak that we become drained.

One of the most extreme stimulations a human being can experience is on the battlefield, and for centuries samurai warriors would come to Zen to learn how to harness this grounding power to perform well within such testing situations. In his *Yasenkana*, Hakuin writes: 'A man who perfectly masters the way always attends to the lower, filling the lower body with his heart energy. If the heart energy fills the lower body, the seven ills cannot operate, nor can the four evils invade.'[6]

You can access this groundedness, power and strength by empowering your legs in combination with the abdominal work we explored in the previous chapter. Establishing this grounding will allow you to harness the energy around you as well as within you, and will give you a strong root to underpin your practice. Following the ancient belief that power or energy follows intention, here you simply bring your intention to fill the abdomen and legs using breath as a vehicle for that intention.

I was taught a version of this work starting in the standing position and then moving to lying down. In his writings, Hakuin doesn't mention the standing, and tells us:

> ...lie down on your back and close your eyes without falling into sleep. Extend your legs out strongly together and draw down the energy of your body to fill the navel, the stomach, the *tanden*, the loins and legs down to the arches of your feet.

---

6 Ekaku, H. *Yasenkana*; see the section '*Yasenkana* (*Night Boat Conversation*) by Hakuin Zenji' in Chapter 13 for the source of this conversation.

In a moment, we'll explore how you draw down the energy in this way. Hakuin then suggests introducing a *koan* to the process. These days, we tend to modify this questioning slightly. After describing the process, Hakuin continues:

> After meditating like this for a week or three weeks, the disharmony of your internal organs, the depletion of your heart and energy, and your physical exhaustion will all be completely cured. If not, you may cut off this old reverend's head.[7]

Let's test his claims...

ENERGISING THE LEGS

You can find a recorded audio version of these instructions online at www.zenways.org/practical-zen-online (the password is 'insight').

As mentioned, I've been taught to start this practice from standing and then lie the body down. Let's try it this way. If necessary, you can begin by sitting. Have your body upright, feet hip-width apart, and notice the connection between the ground and your feet. Feel your toes, the balls of your feet, the outside of your feet, your heels connecting down into the earth, but feel the lift through your insteps or arches.

Have your knees soft, your body upright but not tense, your ears in line with your shoulders, and your

---

7   Ekaku, H. *Yasenkana*; see the section '*Night Boat Conversation* by Hakuin Zenji' in Chapter 13 for the source of these quotations.

nose in line with your navel. Let your breathing be soft and in your belly. Have your hands beside your body and lower your gaze.

Inhale and sweep your arms out to the sides and upwards with a scooping motion, the fingers of each hand almost meeting their counterpart above your head. As you sweep your hands upwards like this, imagine you're scooping up all the energy of the universe into a big ball.

As you exhale, move your hands downwards toward the floor, palms down, drawing all this energy down to fill your belly and legs. As you do this, imagine you are drawing all the energy in your upper body and head downwards too.

Repeat this for 21 breaths, keeping a mental count.

Now lie down and get comfortable with your legs out straight. Duplicate your standing position, but now you're horizontal.

Inhale and move your arms in the same way you did when standing, gathering your energy ball. Exhale and imagine again you're filling your belly and legs. Repeat 21 times.

Now rest your arms by your side, and without any movement, just using your breath and intention, on each in-breath imagine you're inhaling the whole universe. On each out-breath draw this energy down and imagine you're filling your belly and legs. Repeat a further 21 times.

As mentioned above, Hakuin suggests you use a question to draw and keep your attention (and hence your energy) down into your lower body. Many students have found it helpful to mentally ask, 'How is it in my belly and legs?'

By now you'll have developed a feeling for the process. Simply relax and allow it to continue to happen for as long as it takes to reach the 25-minute mark. Then gently sit up and notice how you feel. Many practitioners feel light, released and open in the upper body and full and energised in the lower body.

Spend five minutes writing in your meditation diary. As usual we're just using the diary as a 'brain dump'. Simply write without any attempt at censorship or correctness.

For some people the effects are subtle in the beginning. For others it can be quite the opposite. You'll notice in the *Yasenkana* that Hakuin presents this practice as a prelude to sleep. Don't be surprised if it affects you this way. Many of us need more sleep than we get. Be kind to your body – if you need to sleep, please sleep. Paradoxically, as we begin to restore the body's energy reserves, we may feel more tired than we did before. Over the week, you'll almost certainly feel a restoration. In time you'll find you're more balanced and empowered, more able to deal with difficult or draining situations. Ideally you'll have surplus energy for your spiritual practice to go deeper.

CHAPTER 8

ACTIVITY'S WHEEL RUNS FREE

Cloud gate passed; beyond the old way.
Truly my home is blue sky, bright sun.
Activity's wheel runs free; hard for the people to get.
Golden Kasyapa respectfully leaves.

(*Zen master Daito Kokushi*)[1]

When we've built the energetic root explored in the previous two chapters, what then?

Just for a moment, close your eyes and imagine that your whole upper body and head is completely relaxed. Instead of your normal solidity, imagine the feeling of your body like a fountain, the jet of the fountain running

---

1 Translation by the author and Matt Shinkai Kane. Golden Kasyapa was the Buddha's successor. He respectfully leaves because his teaching isn't needed any more.

up your spine, the spray running over your face and down the front of your body. The more your body relaxes, the more intensely the fountain can flow, ungraspable, yet fully present and utterly alive. Take a few breaths to really sense how this could be. Then open your eyes.

Life is change. As you sharpen your meditative awareness, you start to experience this directly. Anything, no matter how solid, when looked at closely enough, can be seen to be an ungraspable dance. As we become aware of this dance, even within the seeming density of our own body and mind, a transformation is set in progress.

One of my students commented:

'In my meditation, I'm finding things moving from block to flow. Block feels like it sounds – tight, closed and defensive. Flow is open, alive and healthy. It's taken quite an adjustment to realise that the whole world is also flowing like this. As I change inside, so does my view.'

A traditional *koan* has it:

In an undug well
Water ripples from an unflowing spring;
One without shadow or form
Draws the water.

In this chapter we are going to consider this unblocking and re-orientation phase of Zen practice.

Before the Second World War, the term *kensho* was not popular in Zen Buddhism. A term more commonly used was *taitoku*, which can be translated as 'bodily attainment'. If *kensho* is a taste of the unconditioned, a taste of that place beyond the suffering of subject and object, then *taitoku* implies that you have had much more than a taste and have actually eaten the meal – swallowed it, digested it and it has become fully you.

This digestion and embodiment of a new life is fundamental to Zen.

In a classical Zen Buddhist education, once a monk experienced the initial understanding, or opening of the way, he would disappear from public view for a time, during which this transformation could take place. Daito Kokushi, who wrote the poem cited at the beginning of this chapter, matured his understanding by living for years as an anonymous beggar under Gojo Bridge in Kyoto. These days, when a monk has achieved some maturity in his practice, he tends to be given a minor rural temple to look after. Shinzan Rōshi, for example, was given a tiny temple up in Hida, the remote mountainous part of Gifu in central Japan.

When he sent me back to the UK in 2007, Shinzan Rōshi told me to focus on this phase for a while. After I'd walked the length of Britain, I moved to London. For about five years I lived quietly in an unheated, single room. When students came to practise Zen, I would sit outside under an apple tree and they would come individually for their *sanzen* (one-to-one practice interviews). The UK weather, particularly in winter, deterred all but the serious!

When a lay practitioner is going through this stage, he or she might be leading a totally normal life on the outside, completely indistinguishable from anyone else. And yet, inside, a deep spiritual process is under way. Even though sometimes thought of as 'advanced practice', I've found that for many people it's helpful to have a sense of this transformation process from early on in their Zen practice. It helps to dissolve away the view that there's one definitive shift in understanding and then 'happy ever after' eternal bliss.

This phase of practice is traditionally called *shotaicho*, which means 'long nurturing of the sacred embryo'. It is as though the taste of the unconditioned, or *kensho*, is a kind of spiritual impregnation that is nurtured before it matures to full term. You may or may not be at this phase in your life yet. Nevertheless, I believe it's helpful to have the context and the tools to deal with it.

Imagery of this nature can be found throughout the world's mystical traditions. In one of his sermons, the Christian mystic Meister Eckhart writes:

> I once had a dream. I dreamt that I, even though a man, was pregnant; pregnant and full with Nothingness, like a woman is with child. And that out of this Nothingness, God was born... The being and the nature of God are mine... What good is it to me for the Creator to give birth to his Son if I also do not give birth to him in my time and my culture?[2]

This embryo imagery for practice is widespread within Zen in both China and Japan. It developed particularly around the figure of Bodhidharma, considered to be the first Zen ancestor in China. You may have heard that Bodhidharma is said to have meditated for nine years in a cave. Some of the secret Zen documents draw parallels between these nine years

2 Quoted in Fox, M. (1983) *Meditations with Meister Eckhart*. Rochester, VT: Bear & Company, p.78.

and the nine months in the mother's womb. You may have seen pictures of him wrapped in a red robe with only his face exposed, swaddled like a baby.

As mentioned, this process to achieve the condition of matured understanding and embodiment of the truth implies a bodily change. The initial taste or first understanding can be quick, but this maturing cannot be hurried. It develops over the months and years of practice.

In truth, this transformation begins the first time you open your mind to its possibility; the key lies in your attitude of mind. It parallels the way a pregnant woman attends to her unborn child. Sometimes the 'spiritual embryo' is in the foreground of your mind and at others in the background, but it is always there, growing and developing.

Shinzan Rōshi used to say that Zen practice is like learning to play a musical instrument, and as with the finger exercises and scales required, it has a repetitive quality. For long periods of time you may feel as though you are simply going through the motions. Don't be surprised, however, if at some time the motions start to go through you.

Zen master Dogen, the great founder of Soto Zen, alludes to a fable concerning a man named Seiko, who was fascinated by dragons and collected dragon-themed artworks. One day a real dragon thought, 'If I appear in Seiko's house he will be delighted.' But when Seiko saw the dragon, he was absolutely terrified. How about you, are you ready for things to get real? If you practise seriously, the universe will take you seriously.

As your practice starts to come alive in this way, there can be feelings of energy and bliss. These can be a source of attachment and fascination. But if you make them into an object to grasp, they become elusive. One of my Zen teachers used to say, 'You can trail your hand in the mountain stream and enjoy the beautiful experience, but the minute you try to grab a handful to take away, you end up with nothing.' As you learn to open your hands, however, you can tap more and more fully into a source of energy that is inexhaustible.

As we've been exploring, Hakuin teaches that it is wise to first establish and energise the *hara* and then the legs to develop the roots of the tree so that the trunk can grow strong. How do we grow the trunk? We allow the energy to circulate through the trunk of the physical body.

Not every Zen teacher is comfortable with these teachings. Abbot Muho, head of Antaiji, a prominent Japanese Soto Zen temple, writes:

> According to some teachers, meditation will make your *ki*, some kind of vital energy, circulate in your body. Starting in the navel area, the *ki* is supposed to move up the spine, through the neck to the top of the skull, and from there eventually back down the forehead heading towards the breast, and back to the navel... If this explanation makes you happy, good for you. I usually have my doubts about this kind of humbug.[3]

Let's explore this 'humbug'. How can we experience 'activity's wheel runs free', as Daito Kokushi puts it?

A good way into this is via the breath. Spiritual teachings from almost every culture are in agreement that there is a link between the breath and the energetic state of the body. We can breathe in a circle, up the back and down the front.

Of course, the breath doesn't really move in any direction other than in and out of your lungs. What does it mean, then, to follow this circular breathing instruction?

---

3   See http://antaiji.org/archives/201207.shtml

You use the breath as a vehicle for your intention; imagine the breath moving in a circle and usually, in a very short time, you begin to feel something.

As meditation progresses, the breath typically slows down, but in contrast, this 'something' you feel often accelerates and becomes independent of the rhythm of the breath.

One of my teachers compared this process to the use of a crank handle to start an old car. After a certain point the engine roars into life and then all we need do is jump in the car and drive.

There is no way you can hold on to this flow – trying to control it just chokes it down. Our intentionality is best combined with an attitude of acceptance.

There is much more to explore in this area of energetic development, but this circulation practice can begin the unfolding.

When you surrender to the flow and allow it to increase, you can begin to sense what it might mean to nurture the sacred embryo and eventually experience for yourself the blissful time when, 'one morning, the elixir furnace will turn over and everywhere, within and without, will become one great circulating elixir'.[4]

TURNING THE WHEEL OF THE LAW

As we've said previously, when you are working with the energy of the body, the *ki*, wherever your mind or intention goes, the energy follows.

---

4 Ekaku, H. *Yasenkana*; see the section 'Yasenkana (*Night Boat Conversation*) by Hakuin Zenji' in Chapter 13 for the source of this quotation.

By bringing your mind (or attention) to your belly, you charge it up. In the energetic mapping of the East Asian medical and spiritual systems, on which this practice is based, the belly is essentially your battery. You recharge this area, and from here your whole system is recharged.

As with the previous practices, read through first and then follow the practice. Again, you can find a recorded audio version of these instructions online at www.zenways.org/practical-zen-online (the password is 'insight').

Set a timer for 25 minutes.

Establish your meditation posture – either on a chair, kneeling or cross-legged. You'll be very familiar with the alignment by now. Sway a little from side to side, forwards and backwards, to find your position of natural uprightness.

Relax your shoulders; have your neck long with your head directly above your sitting bones. Rest your hands in your lap, on a cushion if necessary. Have your mouth closed with your tongue resting gently on the roof. Allow your eyes to soften and lower, or if you wish, you can close them.

Allow your breathing to be natural and easy. Feel the rising and sinking of the breath deep down in your body, ideally down in your belly. As you bring your focus here, notice how your belly starts to feel strong and powerful.

Now, allow the energy from your belly to overflow into the tip of your spine at the tail area. As you breathe in through your nose, imagine you are breathing energy up your spine, and as you breathe out, imagine you are breathing this energy over your head and down your front to return to the tip of your spine.

Keep your breathing very natural and soft, and allow yourself to experience exactly what you feel. Use your breath to guide your intention: in-breath – from the tip of your spine up your back to your head; out-breath – over your head, down your front and back to the tip of your spine.

Your breath and your awareness will be travelling in a very natural circle. If you find areas that seem tight or restricted, simply hold them in your awareness and allow them to open.

As you breathe in this circular pattern, just be open. It may be that nothing else seems to happen. It may be that you start to feel sensations along this circular course. Sometimes people feel tingling or rushing feelings, or electricity. Sometimes people seem to hear a kind of roaring; some people experience visual effects such as circulating lights, that sort of thing. Don't try to sense anything in particular; just look after the breathing in the circle and allow any results or effects to happen naturally.

As you become more comfortable and relaxed, you may find feelings of movement or flow in the circle circulate faster than your breathing. This happens in much the same way that the wheels on a bicycle can turn faster than its pedals. If this seems to happen, just allow it.

As this circular quality becomes established in your system, you'll feel your whole being integrating and harmonising.

The more you relax, the finer your awareness can become. Feel and explore how things are for you right now. Be aware of places where things can open up further. How are things in your heart? Could things open up more in your solar plexus, the area below your diaphragm? What about the area around the base of your spine?

Keep your basic breathing and intention: in-breath up the back, out-breath down the front. Let everything else look after itself.

At the end of your meditation period, bring your awareness down to your belly and just let everything settle there for a few moments. Then sway your body gently from side to side, and gradually allow your attention to turn to your surroundings once more.

This practice shares much in common with a Taoist practice called the 'microcosmic orbit'. In the Zen tradition I've heard it called *naitan* (literally 'inner elixir').

Expanding the quotation above about circulating elixir, Hakuin draws on traditional alchemical imagery when he writes:

A man needs to draw this energy down and store it in the space below the navel, in the kikai tanden. If he maintains this for months and years without distraction, one morning, the elixir furnace will turn over and everywhere, within and without, will become one great circulating elixir. He will realise that he himself is older than heaven and earth, deathless as space. This is true alchemy. It is not a trivial method for flying in the sky on the wind and mists, or walking on the water. The true immortal can churn the ocean into cream and transform earth into gold.[5]

---

5   Ekaku, H. Yasenkana; see the section 'Yasenkana (*Night Boat Conversation*) by Hakuin Zenji' in Chapter 13 for the source of this quotation.

In the management of this *ki* within the body, we need to be aware that the sense organs can be open gates for energy loss. Hakuin also wrote:

> Frequently people say the divine elixir is the distillation of the five elements, but they are unaware that these five elements, water, fire, wood, metal and earth, are associated with the five sense organs: the eyes, ears, nose, tongue and body. How does one bring together these five organs in order to distil the divine elixir? For this we have the law of the five non-outflowings: when the eye does not see recklessly, when the ear does not hear recklessly, when the tongue does not taste recklessly, when the body does not feel recklessly, when the consciousness does not think recklessly, then the primal energy accumulates before your very eyes.[6]

So, we need to turn the senses within, and this is brought about by a particular attitude of 'attending to the lower', as again explained by Hakuin:

> Generally speaking, essence, energy and spirit are the foundation stones of the human body. The enlightened man guards his energy and does not expend it.
>
> The art of nurturing life can be compared to the techniques of governing a country. The spirit represents the prince, the essence the ministers, and the energy, the people. When the people are loved and cared for, the country is perfected; when the energy is guarded, then the body is perfected. When the people are in turmoil the nation is destroyed; when the energy

---

6   Yampolsky, P.B. (editor and translator) (1971) *The Zen Master Hakuin*. Oretegama I. New York: Columbia University Press, p.42.

is exhausted, the body dies. Therefore the wise ruler always turns his efforts to the common people, while the foolish ruler allows the upper classes to have their way...

The human body is just like this. The enlightened man allows the vital breath to accumulate fully below. Therefore there is no room for the seven misfortunes to operate, nor can the four evils invade from outside. The circulatory organs work efficiently and the heart and mind brim with health.[7]

Hakuin's teachings on energy may not be universally accepted within Zen, but we have records dating back over 500 years of the deeper teachings given during *shotaicho*.

This practice was called *missan* Zen or secret Zen study. In some Zen lineages it still goes on. Exactly what form this secret or private study takes varies from teacher to teacher, but broadly speaking, after the first true understanding, these teachings are given one to one in the master's room. Some of them deal with the maturation of understanding or *taitoku*.

For example, an extract of one historical *missan* text is very clear about Bodhidarma's nine years mentioned previously, and is presented in dialogue form. Question: 'What about the Bodhidarma's nine years before the wall?' Answer: 'These are, in fact, the nine months spent in the womb.'[8]

Another of these ancient secret texts discusses the famous *koan* of 'The man up a tree'.

Master Kyogan said: 'Suppose a man were up a tree. He holds on to a tree branch with his teeth. He can grasp

---

7   Yampolsky, P.B. (editor and translator) (1971) *The Zen Master Hakuin.* Oretegama I. New York: Columbia University Press, p.44.
8   Haskell, P. (2012) 'Bankei and his world: Zen notes.' *First Zen Institute of America LVII*, 2, Spring, p.5.

no branch with his feet and cannot reach the trunk of the tree. Beneath the tree is someone who asks, "What is the meaning of Bodhidarma coming from the west?" If the man does not respond he will fail the questioner's need. If he does answer he will fall to his death. In this situation how should one respond?'[9]

The *missan* Zen text interprets the tree as representing the mother's body, and the man hanging from the tree as the placenta 'sucking the roots of milk' in the womb.[10] In hanging from the tree, the man is, as it were, existing between life and death – exactly the condition of deep meditation and the place in which this transformation can happen.

In my experience, some practitioners have found these secret Zen teachings to simply hold a symbolic meaning representing the maturing of practice. But for others, the teachings have led to very physical results. The practice here is a start in encouraging this energetic rebirth, or regeneration.

These changes may be accompanied by dreams or even visions where different aspects of reality begin to show themselves. Some people experience sensations of tremendous energy moving through the body as though it were being rewired or reprogrammed.

It is possible to block this process, and sadly, through ignorance and fear, this sometimes happens. But generally, if we don't get in the way, the development quietly continues and, like the maturing embryo in the womb, it will eventually take on a life of its own.

---

9   See http://darumasan.blogspot.co.uk/2009/07/red-and-smallpox-essay. html

10 See http://darumasan.blogspot.co.uk/2009/07/red-and-smallpox-essay. html

PART II

THE REST OF YOUR LIFE

CHAPTER 9

BRINGING IT ALL TOGETHER

Just sit upright for a moment. Close or lower your eyes. Find your physical and energetic centre, the *tanden* – the spot in the centre of your body, at a level roughly three fingers' width below your navel. Expanding your awareness from here, establish the grounded energised sense that you're now familiar with. Allow the tree to grow – the energy flowing through your trunk. Come into a condition of presence. You can use the breath or your *koan* to do this, or you can come into this place directly. Enjoy being here for a few minutes.

Over the past 49 days (assuming you've been practising as set out in Part I) we've explored a spectrum of Zen meditation practices. Now we're going to work with developing a combination.

In his retreat instructions, Hakuin writes:

...straighten the spine, settle the body, and begin counting the breath. This practice of counting the breath is the best way to enter into *samadhi*. At this point, fill the *hara* with energy and then bring complete focus to your *koan*. You should resolve with all of your being to maintain this concentration.

Those who continue this sole, unrelenting focus on their *koan* for a period of time will without a doubt experience *kensho*.[1]

To work this combination most successfully, we need to remember Hakuin's image of the two wings of a bird or the two wheels of a cart. These two key elements are:

- *rikan* – practices that help you connect with the truth of things and the happiness that nobody can give you and nobody can take away
- *naikan* – practices that develop a grounded, energised system.

Why do we want this combination? Simply because this gives us the basis for a long, useful, happy life. We'll explore a method of bringing these practices together shortly.

As we start to explore this blending process, I recommend that you continue to practise every day. Aim for 100 days without missing a single day of meditation practice. Later still, you may want to consider two meditation practice periods: morning and evening. You may well get great benefit from more concentrated retreat time as well. Group Zen retreats or *sesshin* can be very powerful, as can some solitary time.

---

1   See the section 'From Hakuin's *Rohatsu Retreat Instructions*' in Chapter 13 for the source of this quotation.

Doing this work of establishing a strong daily habit of meditation practice builds a powerful foundation. Assuming you have this, let's think about another dimension of 'bringing it all together': bringing this work into your daily life.

Automatically, the effects of daily sitting meditation will spill over into your life. But you can help by, in addition to your 'daily dose', finding a few moments of stillness here and there – for example, 'brushing your teeth meditating', or a 'three-minute toilet break meditation'. Better still if you can fit it in a few times a day. Often other people will notice the results before you, or perhaps you start coming across as more patient, or focused, or vital.

While this is all to the good, it's even better to actively explore how to bring the grounding, energy and awareness of your sitting meditation into action, and make your whole life an arena for your practice.

Zen master Hakuin tackles this issue head on when he writes:

> Suppose a man accidentally drops two or three gold coins in a crowded street swarming with people. Does he forget about the money because all eyes are upon him? Does he stop looking for them because he will cause a disturbance? ... A person who concentrates solely on meditation amid the press and worries of everyday life will be like the man who has dropped the gold coins and devotes himself to seeking them. Who will not rejoice in such a person?[2]

---

2   Yampolsky, P.B. (editor and translator) (1971) *The Zen Master Hakuin.* Oretegama I. New York: Columbia University Press, p.49.

You don't need to run away from your life and your responsibilities. In fact, it is good to stay engaged with everything you are doing. However, the manner of your engagement can shift.

Shinzan Rōshi used to distinguish *zazen*, 'practice in stillness', and *do-zen*, 'practice in activity'. Both, he thought, were essential. Zen master Daiye Soko went further. He taught that practice in activity is 10,000 times more valuable than practice in stillness.

When we think of *do-zen* we can divide it into two areas. The first is in solitary activity, and the second is found in our interactions with others. For me, bringing Zen practice into action wasn't so easy. When I was getting started, I was a young corporate animal. In trying to work out what it might mean to practise Zen within the context of my job in the pharmaceutical industry, I received general guidance about being mindful and aware in daily life. Each day I tried to apply this. I tried to focus on what was in front of me. But no matter how hard I tried, all sorts of bustle and busyness swept away what little awareness I was able to muster. I felt I couldn't get a foothold.

After a few frustrating weeks, I decided on a different tack. In the office where I worked there was a little booth with a kettle and tea and coffee. Every morning when I wasn't in a meeting, I would head down there at 10.30 to make myself a cup of tea. I decided to make this my tea break meditation. I began to bring my awareness into the present moment. When I filled the kettle, I just filled the kettle. When I drank the tea, I simply drank.

This morning tea break became an island of relaxed awareness within the maelstrom, and was so pleasurable that repeating it during the afternoon break was easy. Over the following week or two these tea break meditations became a part of life, a habit.

Once these were established, I began to look for other areas in my life where I could meditate. My office building was full of staircases, and several times a day I would run up and down on various errands. This became my staircase meditation – I'd just be as present as I could within the simple activity of walking the stairs. Soon I had five or six islands of mindfulness within the day, and it wasn't long before this began to spread.

When students are developing this everyday awareness, I typically suggest that they track progress in their meditation diaries. Simply recording a guesstimate of what percentage of the time they are able to maintain this awareness is a tremendous spur to developing further.

This kind of concentrating on the present sounds intuitively appealing. Bringing your awareness into the present during these solitary moments is a good place to start and will bring changes to your life. But this is the easy part. The more intense practice (where gains can be realised most powerfully) is in our interactions with other people. Other people are often the source of our deepest joys and our greatest pains, and we need to know how to continue our practice in the context of these relationships.

There is a saying in Zen: 'Buddhas appear troublesomely and ancestors teach in detail.' If you can see the difficult person in front of you as your Buddha of the moment, there is always something you can learn. When someone's actions lead to disquiet or pain within you, that pain is pointing right at the heart of your self and the clinging that is preventing you from realising complete liberation.

So the people around you, particularly the more awkward and obstreperous ones, are wonderful indicators of where things can soften within you, and where you can let go even further. If you can do this, you catapult your practice forward.

This process is, however, not about making yourself into some kind of doormat. It is very important that you are treated well and you treat others well. There are times when the most appropriate response to a situation is a firm 'no'. However, if you can maintain your inner awareness during and after a tough encounter, and can track the responses in your body and mind, just this awareness itself begins to change things. You begin to use the awkward person in front of you to show you where you can let go further, where you can find greater freedom. They unwittingly become your teacher, the Buddha of the moment.

The environment within Zen temples is organised to force monks to use their interactions with others as practice. I mentioned previously the 'rock tumbler' of the meditation hall. When you are with other people for every moment of every day like this, the pressure builds up. There is no escape, and you either have to deal with all the stresses and strains of human interaction, run away, or go crazy. Zen temples are traditionally hard to get into, and this is one good reason why. Many people do take an escape route, and I've seen suicides and attempted suicides result from such stress.

I remember one junior monk in Shinzan Rōshi's temple who disappeared in sub-zero temperatures in the middle of winter. A few days later the police found him sleeping outside by a nearby river. For him the risk of death by exposure was preferable to the pressure of temple life. He came back, tried again, and ended up doing much better.

Once Shinzan Rōshi started to seriously consider me as a candidate to be his successor, he really turned up the heat on me. Even more than usual he filled any empty spaces in the temple with homeless and needy people. I was *fuku jushoku*, or vice-abbot, at the time. Mostly he stood back and watched to see how I got on with bringing in money to keep these people fed, with keeping some sort of order and maintaining the rhythm of practice. I've never been so tested.

Of course, it isn't necessary to live in a temple to take advantage of human frictions. Family life and workplaces do just as well. The point is not to deliberately seek out difficult people and make life hard for yourself, but to develop an attitude whereby you can learn from every situation and every person. There is always the possibility of letting go of the negativities and experiencing greater aliveness and love.

The overwhelming majority of Zen people in Japan are married. Shinzan Rōshi believed that the intensity of interpersonal practice in the monastery should be ideally carried forward into the marriage relationship. He would say, 'Every day husband and wife no escape, like *zendo* life.'

When there's no escape, the best way is forward. As mentioned previously, the scientific research looking at our learning and developmental processes claims that for human beings it takes about 10,000 hours of practice to achieve mastery. As implied previously, with a strong commitment to daily life Zen practice, this 10,000 hours becomes quite an achievable goal. However, although it is possible to attain a deep understanding in your meditation quite quickly, this transformation of the way you live does take time. Traditionally it is seen as the ongoing work of a lifetime.

One way of looking at your life is in terms of its path or way. You may be familiar with the Chinese word *tao*. This can be translated literally as 'road', but it also carries connotations of 'way'. The Japanese version is *do*. So *judo* means 'the gentle way', *sado* is 'the way of tea' (or tea ceremony) and *shodo* is 'the way of the brush'. Each person has some kind of trade or occupation, and over years of inner work and outer experience, he or she gradually attains true mastery of their 'way'.

For us in the modern world this mastery will almost certainly involve activities that are not traditional, and this is a good thing. We may not yet know what an enlightened computer programmer or an enlightened advertising executive looks like, but the potential is clear. Each person, over time, has the possibility of finding and following his or her way.

All of these ways, however they evolve, have two things in common. First, there is a sense of contentment, happiness or bliss about the practice of the way; and second, there is a loosening of the grip of selfhood, out of which arises a quality of service and of helping the greater good. My Zen teachers always emphasised that your way is right in front of your nose. You don't need to make huge gestures and dramatic changes. Rather, it is a matter of engaging with the unfolding moment-by-moment events of your life. And as we have seen throughout this book, focusing on living truly and well right now can allow an extraordinary life to unfold.

Having stressed the value of practice in action, let's return to your sitting place.

COMBINED PRACTICE

As mentioned at the beginning of this chapter, Hakuin Zenji, the great 17th-century reviver of the Rinzai tradition, wanted us to bring together the elements of practice. Over time these separate elements meld together seamlessly and every practitioner evolves his or her own specific recipe, but here we will start the process of developing a meditation practice to sustain and inspire you throughout your whole life.

Get comfortable in your sitting place and allow your whole body to relax. Notice the expansion and release of your breath in your belly, and as you keep your focus, notice how your belly starts to feel strong and powerful.

We will begin with 'ah-un' breathing. You can use the sounds, or do it silently, as is appropriate for you. Without making a sound, draw a deep 'ah' breath in through your nose into your belly, keeping your chest relaxed. Now swallow, lift your perineum and breathe out with a long 'unn' into the front of your belly.

Continue the 'ah-un' breathing now into the sides of your belly and then into the back, remembering to swallow, and lift your perineum between each inhalation and exhalation.

Take a moment to connect with how it feels to be empowered, grounded and centred in your *hara*.

Now draw your attention to the top of your head and imagine a ball of precious healing ointment just resting there. The heat radiating from your head gently melts this ball, and the fragrant ointment flows down over your face. It sinks through your head, your brain and down to your neck, relaxing and cleansing as it flows.

The ointment melts down through your chest and your upper arms, and even as it passes, more ointment pours down over your head. Now it passes down through your body, and all the way down your arms to your hands and fingers, healing and soothing and relaxing. This curing ointment flows steadily down through your belly and your pelvis. And it pours down your legs, into your knees and down to your feet and toes, and as it passes, notice how your whole centre of gravity has moved downwards. Feel how grounded and stable you are in your *hara*; feel how energised and strong you are in your legs.

Now turn your attention to your breathing through your nose. As you inhale, imagine the energy from your *hara* and legs rising up your spine, and as you exhale, imagine it pouring over your head and down the front of your body. Your breath leads your energy in this natural circle, so inhale up your back and exhale down your front. You may find your energy flows much faster than your natural breath in the way a bicycle's wheels can turn faster than its pedals, and you are sitting, relaxing and breathing – you are balancing and recharging your whole system.

Take a moment to sense the grounded and empowered feeling in your lower body and the open flowing quality in your upper body.

And now bring your awareness to your abdomen. Become aware of the natural, soft, rising and falling with each breath. Rest your attention on the *tanden* point, on a level roughly three fingers' width below the navel in the centre of your body, and then begin to count. As you inhale, mentally count 'one', as you exhale count 'two', and so on up to ten, and then start again at one. Stay with your breath. Any time you lose count, just begin again at one. And you may find as you breathe, count and relax that things become very deep; and as things become deep your breathing may become very light and very slow.

Now let your awareness expand from your breath to encompass all things. Your awareness is a great, round mirror, and you are just resting in this mirror-like awareness. Allowing anything at all to rise and anything at all to pass away, you just rest with an open presence. And any time you notice yourself identifying with one thing or another, thinking about something or remembering something, this attention will automatically bring you back to your open, mirror-like awareness. If you wish, you can rest here as long as you like, even through your whole life.

Or, if you wish, you can turn all your faculties, your senses, within, and ask yourself silently, 'Who am I?' Look within. Explore and investigate; allow your whole attention to focus on this question – who am I? Many different answers and theories may arise, but know that the reality of your being is so much more than any theory. Bring the doubting into your belly and allow it to crystallise there, and all the while you are searching and questioning and keeping this question as your focal point through your meditation.

And as you come to the end of this meditation period you can keep this question with you. In your busy times let it settle in the back of your mind, and in your quiet times draw it to the front of your awareness and let it settle in your belly. Great master Hakuin called this 'a ball of doubt', so allow this ball of questioning to form in your belly. And as you steadily and assiduously focus on this question, know that the time will come, probably sooner than you think, when your door of enlightenment will burst open and you will know who you truly are.

I suggest using your meditation time going forward as an opportunity to explore blending these practices. Using your meditation diary and your intuitive sense of things, sense what is particularly needed or helpful. You may find at times that you just want to focus on one or two of the practices; at other times you may want to include all of them. Treat them as a toolkit. You've learned to use these tools, so now enjoy the combinations.

You may find your personal blend naturally evolves and stabilises. You may find things are different every day. Either way is fine. You may also want to explore sitting for longer than 25 minutes, or finding two meditation spaces within your day. Regardless of the specifics, I recommend maintaining your meditation diary.

Over the centuries, the Zen tradition has found that it is beneficial to have retreat periods when you can go all out and throw your whole being into formal meditation. Most of the time, however, it is more effective to practise in a way that is sustainable in the long term, emphasising continuity rather than dramatic, exaggerated efforts. Do what you can to establish this powerful, and yet unobtrusive, continuity.

CHAPTER 10

ROADMAPS FOR YOUR JOURNEY

If you decide to use these practices to set out on a spiritual path, the details of your journey will be unique to you. In many ways it is a road of adventure – perhaps the last great adventure available to us on this earth!

No one can take this journey for you, and sometimes the going can get tough. It is possible to meander along the way and waste time dithering or going off on tangents. Conversely, there are no short cuts.

While walking the way is down to you, a competent teacher will save you time. In addition, you can save time by having the guidance of a roadmap. These roadmaps of the journey of spiritual insight occur in most spiritual traditions. If you look beneath the varying imagery, you'll find they have much in common.

If you have connections with a particular religion, you may find it helpful to explore its particular roadmap. Christians, for example, may find it helpful to look into the works of Saint John of the Cross, particularly *The Ascent of Mount Carmel* and *The Dark Night of the Soul*. Alternatively there is an anonymous 14th-century English text called *The Cloud of Unknowing* that is practical, clear and written by someone who clearly knew the ground he describes. In the Muslim tradition there is Ibn Arabi's *Journey to the Lord of Power: A Sufi Manual on Retreat.* There are other works of this kind.

In Zen there is a tradition of using sequences of pictures to depict the stages along the path. Of these, the ox or bull-herding pictures are well known, and here we will examine a version of them from a Zen master called Kakuan from the 12th century.[1] For those coming from other spiritual traditions, or no tradition at all, the ox-herding pictures are approachable, as they are light on overtly religious imagery. What does the ox represent? You could say the forces of life itself.

We'll also refer to the classical Buddhist text, the *Vishuddhimagga* or *The Path of Purification,* for the detailing of some of the stages. Among other writers you'll find many differing interpretations of the ox-herding stages. There is little consensus. The one I detail below corresponds most closely with my own experience, and that of both my teacher and my students.

In the following the ox-herding drawings are by one of my students, Alex Kofuu Reinke.

1. THE SEARCH FOR THE OX

This is the genuine start of practice. At some point in life you become very aware that something is missing. Students come to Zen from all walks of life and for all sorts of reasons, but in my experience there are three main triggers or catalysts that set people off on the path.

---

1   The Buddha himself had used ox-herding imagery centuries before in the *Maha-gopalaka Sutta* (*The Greater Discourse on the Cowherd*).

The first is suffering. People who have experienced deep pain in their lives may urgently need to find some kind of resolution. Shinzan Rōshi himself came to Zen after a whole series of personal disasters and a failed suicide attempt.

Second, some students have experienced another kind of disillusionment. Very often they've come from a successful background, with many of the trappings and symbols that our society associates with success. These things may be enjoyed and there may be a sense of gratitude, but these people are still consumed by a nagging sense that there must be more to life.

And finally, there are those who, perhaps completely unbidden, have had some kind of spiritual awakening or experience that spurs them on to develop further.

Of course, it may be that none of these apply to you and other reasons have brought you to Zen. Regardless of your initial motivation, when you are at this first stage, you have already gone further than just dipping a toe in the water. By now you have made a definite engagement or commitment to your spiritual quest, and there can be a great sense of potential at this stage. The Zen master Shunryu Suzuki talked about having a 'beginner's mind'[2] – the state of open,

2   Shunryu, S. (1970) *Zen Mind, Beginner's Mind*. New York and Tokyo: Weatherhill.

untrammelled awareness. Sometimes there is considerable joy present and a feeling of being, at last, on the path.

The great Zen master Dogen wrote, 'To study Buddhism is to study the self; to study the self is to forget the self.' In this first stage we are studying the self, both mind and body. We begin to realise that ultimately we are not our mind and our body. Sometimes reality can be experienced as very alive and vivid during this stage as perceptions become particularly open and clear. Occasionally a student might think that this aliveness is the goal and that they've already made it. But of course the road continues.

This quality of investigation or exploration can flower into what many Zen masters call 'the great doubt' (*daigidan* in Japanese). In this state, the enquiry takes on an energy or life of its own, even a physicality. Hakuin often refers to forming the great doubt into a ball and placing it in the belly. He writes, 'At the bottom of great doubt lies great awakening.'[3]

2. DISCOVERING THE FOOTPRINTS

Sooner or later the exhilaration of setting out on our quest gives way to the reality of life on the road. In the image characterising this stage, the footprints of the ox represent traces left behind from the past. Teachings from past practitioners can guide you, but

---

3   Yampolsky, P.B. (editor and translator) (1971) *The Zen Master Hakuin.* Oretegama I. New York: Columbia University Press, p.144.

more directly, your body and mind is a living record of the effects of your previous actions and choices. These footprints manifest at many levels of being and experience. Some of these may be of positive emotions such as happiness, but many of us will also experience the negative manifestations.

As the study of the self deepens, the relationship between physical and mental phenomena is perceived directly. We realise in a very clear way that everything – objects, people, emotions – continually changes. Everything has a degree of instability and so can never fully or permanently satisfy us.

The blue sky is not blue, the white clouds are not white.
(Daito, 1282–1336)[4]

The footsteps of the ox are discovered in a physical way too. All kinds of tensions and misalignments caused by the stresses and strains resulting from our past choices can come up into conscious awareness. When I first went through this stage I found my whole body to be a mass of tensions, with particular tightness in my neck and shoulders, my belly and my throat.

This stage can be thought of as a purification or spiritual detox. The Zen term for this is *sange* (pronounced san-gay). If you are willing and open, unskilful things you have done will be perceived, and from this you can learn how to create a better future for yourself and others. As you do this there is a sense of lightening the load.

Over the years I have found many Zen students are shocked to discover how much the past is affecting them. Rather than face up to this uncomfortable reality, some people are tempted

---

4   Quoted in Kraft, K. (1992) *Eloquent Zen*. Honolulu: University of Hawaii Press, p.136.

to simply give up and allow unawareness to take over again. This is a shame because, if we just trust the process and allow whatever needs to arise to do so without holding on or pushing away, things can start to really turn a corner.

3. PERCEIVING THE OX

If we don't give up, the view eventually begins to clear. Our meditation begins to take on a life of its own. Reality might be seen as a network of very fine vibrations, and strong feelings of bliss and a renewed sense of focus can arise. Sometimes there are beautiful experiences of light and visions. And as a lot of energy can be released  in the body, students can feel more vigorous and younger.

It is possible to again feel that you have made it to the end of the journey, with these visions of the grandeur and fundamental beauty of reality. But you have only caught sight of the ox, and there is much further yet to go.

Some people can get really stuck at this level. The *Lotus Sutra* likens this to an image of an unreal city. If we think of ourselves as on a long and arduous journey, this stage is a mirage-like city where we can rest and gather strength. But the quest is by no means over and, just as the magical city appeared, it can also vanish.

The classical way to cause this vanishing is to try to grasp on to the experience itself. The whole path is about opening your hands and letting go. It is utterly natural to get stuck by trying to hold on to experiences. Eventually, however, we get to the point where we realise that all experiences arise and pass – that is their nature. However exalted it seems, no experience is exempt from this iron law.

If we keep practising earnestly, however, the next stage can begin to open up.

4. CATCHING THE OX

Here we are back on the road of purification. Compared to the second stage where the footprints of the ox were seen, this stage, where we actually lay hands on the ox, may feel a lot rougher. Here you come face-to-face directly with the suffering from your past. Most people find this part of the journey hardest to deal with, so  I'm going to write more about this stage than any of the others.

As mentioned before, everyone has their unique journey and burden from their history. So some will pass through this stage quite easily, whereas for others it can be very tough.

Either way, it is important to keep going with the practice once you've reached this level. By this point there have been glimpses of some of the truth of reality, both the suffering and the bliss, and even if the practice is stopped, the suffering is likely to continue. This suffering can take on an existential quality that affects our worldview, so we may feel more intensely than before that we are strangers in a strange land, homeless and lost in the universe. Zen master Mumon referred to this state when he wrote, 'Those who have not passed the barrier and have not cast away the discriminating mind are all phantoms haunting trees and plants.'[5]

It can be hard to come face-to-face with this suffering. No wonder many turn aside. As you go through this stage of catching the ox, profound physical, emotional and mental discomfort, and dis-ease, can arise. It is important not to get involved in the storylines your mind may generate during this stage of the journey. The mind can be extraordinarily ingenious in fabricating reasons why we should turn back and give up on our quest. As T.S. Eliot put it, 'Human kind cannot bear very much reality.'[6]

We can find ourselves worrying about becoming mad or losing our place in society. On my first time through this I found myself terrified that I would lose all usefulness as a person. But perhaps the deepest fear for many is that if the curtain is pulled aside, we will discover we are fundamentally inadequate. Even the Buddha himself faced this sense of unworthiness.

There is only one way through this, and that is to doggedly continue to practise. I've found several things can help. First, it's useful to appreciate that this is only a phase. Like the second stage, here the process is one of deep spiritual detoxification. If you have experienced a physical detox, you'll know it can feel pretty rough as the toxins are washed away, but afterwards you feel absolutely wonderful for months. This process we are considering has many parallels but goes much deeper than the

---

5   Quoted in Shibayama, Z. (2011) *The Book of Mu.* Boston, MA: Wisdom Publications, p.87.
6   Eliot, T.S. (1968) 'Burnt Norton.' In *Four Quartets.* New York: Mariner Books, 20 March.

second stage. Just do your best to keep what's happening in context. Second, having contact with a teacher or peers who understand what you're dealing with can be incredibly helpful. And third, broadening your perspective can make a difference. You may well be doing this for yourself, and that's fine. But if you extend your motivation to practise for the benefit of a loved one, for your family, or even for all beings, the whole process can seem more worthwhile.

When considering what helps, it's useful to remember that the Buddha taught that the happiness of *nirvana* or liberation can be found through:

- mindfulness of the body
- mindfulness of sensations
- mindfulness of the mind
- mindfulness of mind objects.

You can see how these objects of mindfulness break down into two groups: mindfulness of the body and what is going on in the body, and mindfulness of the mind and what is going on in the mind.

Now, the Buddha taught that if we practise mindfulness of any one of these four we can find liberation. In other words, deal with any one and suffering on all four levels is resolved.

For myself, at this stage of catching the ox, I found it helpful to switch my attention towards the physical phenomena arising within me rather than the mental storylines, and I usually recommend this to my students.

There are specific obstacles that can appear at this stage. They vary from person to person, and, as mentioned, having a teacher who has gone through this journey before is a great help. It is normal for fear, anger and confusion to come up, and in the Buddhist analysis, these are seen as the three basic obstacles. Simply try to be as present as possible with the actual embodied experience of the feelings, and allow them to arise and pass.

Some people reach a point in which nothing is happening and there seems only a vast wasteland. If this is the case for you, it is still very important to just keep on with the practice.

5. TAMING THE OX

Essentially the process at this stage is one of de-identifying. Up to this point in life we have been unconsciously identified with our thoughts, feelings, body and experiences. Through this de-identification we can begin to realign with who we really are.

The snow melts and the
bones of the mountain appear. (Daito, 1282–1336)[7]

This experience of catching and taming the ox can vary a lot. Some people have a very gentle ox to deal with, but for others it is wild, and the whole experience can be as intense as a rodeo. With my students I recommend a steady discipline at a measured pace so that the process is manageable. Going

---

7   Quoted in Kraft, K. (1992) *Eloquent Zen*. Honolulu: University of Hawaii Press, p.116.

through this period, some of my students have benefited from psychotherapy in parallel with their Zen practice.

This is a stage when many, or perhaps even most, people give up. Some maintain the appearance and routine of practice, but the quest is abandoned and this really is a shame. Even if you have a wild ox to catch, all that abundant vitality will be available for positive uses if only you can keep going. Be reassured that what you're experiencing is simply a stage and will surely come to an end.

When it does, we reach a stage of equanimity. The ox is tamed. There is sufficient de-identification from all the emotional, physical and mental 'stuff' that it can arise and pass away quite freely.

There is no longer a struggle and absolutely no doubt that the only way is to stay with the practice. With this realisation comes a quality of relief. It may be that some of the suffering still continues to arise, but the crucial shift is that we don't identify with it so much – we don't take it personally. The ox comes to realise that our intentions truly are for the best: our intention is not to kill the ox. With this realisation we become able to lead the ox; we're friends.

I watch the birds fly off at dawn and return home at dusk.[8]

6. RIDING THE OX HOME

The boy and the ox are together. Not quite one, but almost. The experience of this stage can be pleasant. Our view has

---

8   Hori, V.S. (2003) *Zen Sand: The Book of Capping Phrases for Koan Practice.* Honolulu: University of Hawaii, p.580.

shifted, and it may be possible to perceive and ride the vibrating, dynamic, ungraspable reality of things without any particular effort. We can feel like we are sustained by the energy of the universe.

> Measuring with hand-beats the pulsating harmony, I direct the endless rhythm. (Kakuan, 12th century)[9]

The mind is now well trained. When working with a *koan* or other object of meditation, it can be held more or less continuously, but there is still the subtlest sense of distinction between you and your object of meditation – the subtlest sense of you and your ox.

It is possible to ignore this gap and decide the work is done, but with an honest and clear eye, it is obvious there is further to go. The trouble may be that it is not entirely clear how to proceed. You may feel your state is now aligned with the way, but it is nevertheless not quite the way. Being so close means we lose perspective. We can't quite see what to do, and this loss of perspective can be disorientating.

Some students experience this stage as rather like travelling on a train track that is parallel to the track they wish to be on.

---

9   Senzaki, N. and Reps, P. (1957) *Zen Flesh, Zen Bones: A Collection of Zen and Pre-Zen Writings*. North Clarendon, VT: Charles E. Tuttle Inc., p.143.

There seems to be no convergence, and the question is: how can this final gap be crossed?

7. THE OX TRANSCENDED

As always, the way forward is to let go. At a certain point the ox just disappears. This is because you have become one with it. Although this oneness may be a pleasant experience for some, it can also feel like a desert. It can feel as though you are identified with nothing.

Above, no supports for climbing; below, self is extinguished. (Daito, 1282–1336)[10]

The famous Zen text, the *Mumonkan* (*The Gateless Gate*), says: 'All the illusory ideas and delusive thoughts accumulated up to the present will be exterminated, and when the time comes, internal and external will be spontaneously united. You will know this, but for yourself only, like a dumb man who has a dream.'

This stage can have a quality of potential about it, a sort of spiritual pregnancy. This is the end of the line, and you now know what mystics of the past have called 'spiritual poverty'.

---

10 Quoted in Kraft, K. (1992) *Eloquent Zen*. Honolulu: University of Hawaii Press, p.199.

No road to advance on; no gate to retreat through. (Daito, 1282–1336)[11]

The 14th-century meditation manual, *The Cloud of Unknowing*, puts it beautifully:

Let go this everything and something, in preference for this nowhere and this nothing. Do not worry if your senses have no knowledge of this nothing; I love it much the better for this.[12]

But even this nothing is not an end.

8. BOTH OX AND SELF TRANSCENDED

One of my teachers once told me that it is impossible to stay in the previous state for very long without this succeeding stage appearing. But all of that is out of our hands. You don't get to decide when your spiritual pregnancy comes to term.

Before the fullness of this stage arises, there may well be precursors. By no means does everybody experience them, but you may find yourself entering deep states of letting go.

---

11 Quoted in Kraft, K. (1992) *Eloquent Zen*. Honolulu: University of Hawaii Press, p.202.
12 Unpublished manuscript translation, Daizan.

Either gradually or suddenly, you let go of your perception of things being a certain fixed way – you let go of your thoughts and feelings, and even your senses, and seem to go through a certain threshold.

Typically this letting-go state, *samadhi* as it's often called, is deeply restful and beautiful, even blissful. You emerge with your senses, your whole being, purified. This experience of deep letting go is powerful and transforming, but only temporarily so. There is an afterglow of clarity and presence, but it wears off.

The direction you are heading towards is an even further letting go. You, yourself, can't actually do it, but all the inner work you've done up to this point establishes a momentum. You simply keep going, and at a certain point, often when you least expect it, it happens.

And when it happens there is absolutely nothing left, it's a complete discontinuity. Unlike previous *samadhi* experiences, which can last for extended periods, even several hours, this experience is momentary. We die and are reborn in a moment. It's like the lights blink off and then come on again.

Almost any stimulus can bring this about. Zen master Hakuin heard an unexpected bell. Bankei smelt plum blossom. Whatever the immediate stimulus, we are suddenly plunged into what the Bible calls 'The valley of the shadow of death'.

The image of this stage is an *enso*, the famous Zen empty circle. Suddenly reality disappears and so do you. Zen calls it 'the great death'.

Everything is let go, and in this abandoning, there is no time, space or anything else. In discussing this nothing-and-nowhere place, the traditional commentary to the ox-herding picture states, 'Whip, rope, person and bull – all merge into a no-thing.'

9. REACHING THE SOURCE

This is a stage of rebirth. We become a new being in a new world. This rebirth isn't a one-time event; it's happening moment by moment. The idea of a fixed, permanent self is simply laughable.

This stage is often filled with bliss and relief. Sometimes tears of joy and gratitude are shed, and sometimes tears and laughter occur at the same time. We know we are home, and paradoxically we know we always were.

The commentary here states, 'The river is green and the mountain is blue.'[13] Everything is as it is, and embodies a quality of perfection. As with all emotions, those released by this rebirth are passing and transient.

> The capital is a pleasant place, but it's difficult to live there long. (Daito, 1282–1336)[14]

Although it's common for there to be an emotional release at this stage, particularly the first few times we end up here, sometimes our arrival is very quiet. If we can understand that our destination isn't an experience so much as a shift in the

---

13 The Japanese tend to see rivers as green and mountains as blue. In the West we often think of the colours the other way round.

14 Quoted in Kraft, K. (1992) *Eloquent Zen*. Honolulu: University of Hawaii Press, p.205.

way we relate to all experiences, we are less likely to be misled by a temporary elation.

However joyful the emotions released, it is always a mistake to try to hold on to them. Our journey continues.

10. RETURNING TO THE WORLD

*It's over, the Buddhas
and Patriarchs' disease
That once gripped my
chest.
Now I am just an
ordinary man
With a clean slate.*

(Daito, 1282–1336)[15]

In the final picture of the series, the young seeker has become the fat, jolly, laughing Buddha. Here, he is passing on 'The Way' to the next young seeker.

The product of all this spiritual work is not just realisation. This understanding has to be lived and it is natural to want to help others. How life is lived becomes vastly important. The traditional commentary says, 'I visit the wine shop and the market, and everyone I look upon becomes enlightened.'

At some point comes the important realisation that this long journey is actually a cycle and our understanding still isn't complete. The conversation between the laughing Buddha

---

15   Quoted in Kraft, K. (1992) *Eloquent Zen*. Honolulu: University of Hawaii Press, p.191.

and the aspirant seeker goes on internally, as well as in our interactions with others.

Even the sharpest sword must always be re-sharpened. (Rinzai, 866 CE)[16]

There is further to go, and in time the cycle is begun again. Only now the landmarks are more familiar. Every single step of the way requires all our spiritual cards on the table. The work still requires courage and resolution, and it is always possible to stop moving on. But at least we have done it before; we know it in our blood and bones: 'If we can discard a thing as small as our self, then we can experience a thing as large as the Universe.'[17]

Many times in the interview room I remember Shinzan Rōshi miming casting something behind himself and saying to me in English, 'Get and throw, get and throw.' Each understanding must be cast away or it becomes an obstacle to the next. We end up with nothing. Again, in the interview room, I remember him talking through the cost of Zen practice and summing it up in English: 'In the end we become good man, everybody like.'

As our practice continues to deepen, more and more suffering is dealt with, and we become more able to live fearlessly and enjoy our lives. We find a happiness that does not depend on any circumstances. Our life becomes truly beneficial to others.

---

16 Kononenko, I. and Kononenko, I. (2010) *Teachers of Wisdom*. Pittsburgh, PA: Dorrance Publishing, p.159.

17 Koho, K.C. (2000) *Soto Zen*. Mount Shasta, CA: Shasta Abbey Press, p.17.

We have a Japanese term, *intoku*, meaning 'unobtrusive or secret goodness'. This is a sign that practice is truly maturing. When 'Thundering Settan' (1801–1873) was master of my teacher's training monastery, freshly washed and cut vegetables would mysteriously appear in the kitchen every morning. In seeking the perpetrator, Settan Rōshi disguised himself as a monk meditating by night on the mountain. He followed a young *unsui* (training monk) called Tairyu down to the nearby river and watched him gather leaves discarded by local farmers. At that time, Settan Rōshi thought to himself, 'This monk will be my successor.' In the course of time, Tairyu became the next Zen master of Shogengji.

Perhaps this sounds a difficult path. Like all things, some have an affinity for it and an easier time, while others have more to deal with along the way. The truth of the matter is that learning to let go can be done little by little. You can set the pace. When you let go a little, you'll find life gets a little better. When you let go a lot, life gets a lot better!

And of those who have genuinely experienced this rebirth, I've never heard of a single dissatisfied customer.

CHAPTER 11

PUTTING IT INTO PRACTICE

Case Studies

Zen practice works best in the context of community. Working from a book, you're most likely in a solitary situation. I therefore interviewed a selection of Zenways students who had been working with these practices for some time. I aimed for a spread of ages, sexes and backgrounds. Hopefully there's someone you might identify with. I'm hoping that these accounts can give you a sense of what is possible and how life might unfold if you continue with the work.

ED EVANS: 'IT'S HERE! YOU'VE ALREADY GOT IT'

I had a longstanding interest in Japan and I think that led me to Zen. After school I went to RADA, the drama school, and, when I was about 22, I started practising Zen meditation under the influence of the book, *Zen Mind, Beginner's Mind*.[1]

---

1   Suzuki, S. (1970) *Zen Mind, Beginner's Mind* (edited by Trudy Dixon). New York: Weatherhill.

I remember one time not long after I'd started practising: I was meditating outside on Hampstead Heath in London and there was a strong intention to just be. All of a sudden, I found myself utterly aware and utterly at peace. I don't know how long it lasted, but it gave me a proof that this stuff worked.

Eventually, about five years ago, I connected with the Zenways London group, and meeting the Zen students I was very struck how everyone seemed so present. So I jumped right in and began to practise with Daizan Rōshi.

In some ways the Zen group felt like an extension of drama school. I was looking for the spontaneity that the great performers have. The space of *sanzen* – the one-to-one Zen interview – seemed familiar, and I felt that entering this space would help my acting. Since then, right through the transition from drama school and into the world of professional acting, I've been contemplating the relationship of acting and Zen.

Over that time, I've done quite a lot. Quite early on I got to play in 'Twelfth Night' at the National Theatre. I've done TV adverts for Subway, Intel, Barclays and 118118, which have really helped to pay the rent. I did a French drama and also got to play Benjamin Britten at the Royal Opera House. More recently I was in a play on BBC Radio Three called 'Courtly Love'.

One thing I've noticed during this transition: I used to be terrified before going on, but I just don't get nerves any more. On top of that I'd say there is greater emotional availability combined with increased focus and spontaneity.

Looking back, a big shift for me was about a year ago, shortly after Rohatsu (the Buddha's enlightenment retreat), when we'd sat in meditation all night. I was sitting in my room in *zazen* with a clear head. My *koan* was effortlessly present. I suddenly realised: 'It's here! You've already got it. It's right here.' And then it was as if I was gone for a moment and, as I emerged, I knew I was the centre and all phenomena were coming from me. There was no drama; it was all very quiet. But a new perspective seems to have started from there, and it's been growing on me.

And then some time later, I was on retreat. Very quickly on arriving I was engaging with the *koan* and strong emotional stuff started arising, and then it settled down again. I began feeling a lot of frustration and then by the third day it shifted.

I was in a place where I found myself saying things like: 'I am the universe. This is it! I swear to God, this is it. How could anything be added to or removed from this?', and generally saying that I was free and there was no separation.

I questioned myself – could I be absolutely sure this was the truth? I grew up in a family that was atheist and very sceptical. I had a general aversion to spiritual language and religious forms. Finding myself saying with complete conviction things that are the polar opposite of what I could have ever imagined was amazing. I used to think of myself as a human being that knows things and doesn't know other things. Yet, when I connect with this, I have nothing, and then out of this nothing these convictions come out. The question of belief just doesn't arise.

What I'd expected from Zen practice was that you'd strain for years, and eventually you'd explode into light and then life would be rosy forever. For me it's not been quite like that. I thought I'd find a fixed state of happiness, but actually it feels more like I'm in a different way of being, a way of living, and it's not just for me. I feel like there's a responsibility for others within this that I hadn't expected.

My experience has been that fundamentally Zen is about dropping off or letting go. I'd read the books that say this beforehand, but it's only through the practice that I've found that you get nothing and it really is wonderful. And also now I have a faith (and that's not a word previously in my vocabulary) that everything is in hand, that the universe steps up to the plate when you need it to – a non-personal force is somehow underlying it all.

In dealings with others I'd say there is a greater ease with people and also a sense of charisma. This process has a powerful integrity, and I've noticed that other people pick up on that and it gives you a natural authority. I think I'm pretty empathetic as well, but that was probably there before.

My practice continues. Sometimes life gets very happy and it's almost a bit too much because it feels so profound that I can't easily talk about it. Other times I'm feeling unhappy but I can just ride it out and it doesn't seem to knock me over. There is so much more than the rise and fall of any feeling-state. What is that more? Truth be told, I can't really get a grasp on it. Perhaps it's ever thus.

KIM BENNETT: 'IT WAS SO SIMPLE. EVERYTHING I'D BEEN LOOKING FOR WAS *HERE*'

After a period of serious drinking and some very unhelpful relationships, I managed to stop everything. However, I was left with a curtain of despair and darkness. I would have spells, sometimes lasting a day, sometimes up to four or five days, when I couldn't leave the house. My mind would be developing incredible ways to kill myself, and I didn't trust myself not to act on them. I was taken over by anger and self-loathing and a deep sense of 'Is life really worth living with this?' By the time I would get to the third or fourth day of dealing with one of these episodes, I would be utterly exhausted.

There was a definite physicality to these emotions. They would seep through my body like ink through blotting paper. The doctor prescribed me Valium, and I found that when the blackness started coming I could take the Valium and sleep, and when I woke up I'd be okay. So that really helped. But the whole business was paralysing and I felt far from living a normal life.

I began practising Zen meditation. I went on a couple of retreats and took up a daily practice. After I'd been meditating for about nine months I realised that I'd had only two blackness episodes over that time. This was really curious. I hadn't expected meditation to do this, but I couldn't see any other cause. Nothing else had worked, but this gave me some strength and hope.

My normal reaction to feeling the blackness coming was to panic. Now I got to the point where I was fed up with being a victim. The Zen meditation, particularly the Unborn practice (see Chapter 3), gave me the power to stop doing everything, and completely and utterly focus my attention on this thing. So, as one particular episode developed, I just watched these feelings. For hours and hours, I just sat watching and watching. Eventually I fell asleep and it's never come back since. I have occasional blue days, but nothing out of the ordinary.

I wanted to go on holiday. I was looking for somewhere safe and couldn't find where that would be. I'd been drinking for so long. Once I'd stopped the drink and the mad relationship stuff there was a terrifying period when I realised that no one's here to rescue me: it's down to me.

I thought, 'Well, what do I want to do? I love people, I love the sun.' I had the idea of sharing a safe place where you could be sober and single, a place based in meditation. I thought, 'Let's give it a go and see what happens.' And so Serenity Retreat, my holiday company in Greece, was born.

The year I launched, I really didn't know what I was doing. I was very keen that meditation was part of it. So for the trial run I had my first 'guests' (who were actually friends) sit in the meditation position with their eyes closed and I'd have a guided meditation on my iPod plugged into my ear and I just repeated what was said. Fortunately no one noticed. As time has gone on meditation has become even more central to Serenity Retreat.

In terms of my own practice, I remember the first Zen retreat I went on. When the retreat started I mentally went round the room and judged absolutely everyone there. The teacher talked about the sixth Zen ancestor and his teaching about the mind being like a mirror. During the practice I went right through the mirror and realised there wasn't anything to hold on to. My judgement melted. I mentally went round the room giving each person a hug and I came away with a sort of peace.

Since I was already guiding meditation at Serenity Retreat, I felt I needed some formal training. I wanted to be able to speak with conviction to my students. So I came on the Zenways mindfulness and meditation training. I trusted Daizan immediately and that was important to me. I really enjoyed the immersive retreat style of the course, the techniques, the breadth of knowledge, the tradition, the no-nonsense common sense, 'This is what you do, off you go', approach. I loved all of that.

So then I started teaching in earnest. Now I teach Zen meditation every week when I'm in Greece, and it's really a key part of what we do. I'm now into year five of Serenity Retreat and we're on the *Sunday Times* best holiday list, and every single holiday group that comes has Zen meditation. Everything we do as a company comes from the place of meditation.

Back to my own journey. For some time, I'd been working with the *koan* 'Who am I?' I went to Japan and spent some time studying with Shinzan Rōshi. He emphasised bringing the question into activity, into absolutely everything I did. It became almost like a tape running in the back of my mind, and as the question settled in, my reactions to things changed massively. I really noticed this when I nearly missed my flight out of Japan. I found myself just watching it all happening. I thought, 'If I miss it, it's going to be inconvenient, that's all. It doesn't matter that much.' I couldn't believe I was thinking like this.

Back in the UK I was in London on my way to meet with my teacher, Daizan Rōshi. I remember waiting on a Tube platform feeling very calm and loving the city, the madness and intensity of it – so different to Greece, where I spend half the year. And then I was sitting on the Tube train and suddenly I became the question. I was the question. Everything in that moment was the question and everything released. It was so simple. Everything I'd been looking for was *here*.

This was a big shift for me. Since then I've seen how in every reaction I have infinite possibilities. I can bring something new to everything. There's this huge freedom and expansion. There's no beginning, middle and end. I now spend much more time in the present moment and, on the one hand, things get done much more conscientiously, and at the same time I know there's no better and worse. I just get on with it. I don't take it all so seriously. I feel like the battle is over. I feel in my deepest being that the sense of 'me against the world' is just not there any more.

Practice continues. I'm working with another *koan* now. I still have a curiosity about this whole business. I've seen this deep thing that my teacher has and other people have, and I have it too. And still I know I have a choice in each moment to align myself with this or not.

My sitting meditating goes more easily. My ability to stay with things, good and bad, has increased. My ability to enjoy the moment has vastly increased. These days I find I'm more drawn to physical practices such as walking meditation. I simply can't be the same as I used to be. There's this nowness; this is it. So everything has changed and nothing has changed. And the way leads on.

CHRIS OWEN: 'AN ENORMOUS SENSE OF BEING UNBURDENED'

I met Daizan Rōshi and began Zen study just over five years ago. I was a 50-something-year-old city lawyer, head of the corporate part of my firm. The recession had just hit. I had three kids and my eldest was just off to university.

I suppose what attracted me to Zen was my underlying sense that 'there must be more to life'. I'd achieved quite a bit. Society would consider me a success. The family was in good shape. But still I had a general urge to explore.

It was clear I needed to pursue this investigation in the context of my family and responsibilities, and that's how it's been. Since I began my Zen study, I've meditated literally every single day and been on retreat once or twice a year.

To make this work I've found it best to get up an hour earlier. I do a few warm-up exercises and some bows, then half an hour *zazen* meditation. Then, after my shower, I do seven or eight minutes of Zen yoga.

I have always been a do-er. The people I'm mostly surrounded by are similar. By contrast, my Zen practice has emphasised the quality of being.

I've noticed the effects of my practice on different levels. Over the five years I've got a huge amount of insight into myself, into who I am, and a better understanding of why I do what I do. I've done a lot of facing the emotions and pressures that I feel. There's still a long way to go: a while back my family nicknamed me 'The angry Buddhist' – I don't get away with much.

I've seen how my personality type of 'head down and plough on' previously tended to narrow my worldview. There's now a broader, softer, connected view of what is in front of me. So, when I face difficult people, I see how some of that difficulty comes from my responses. I've really gained a lot from the teaching of considering a difficult person to be your teacher of the moment. I can be more open, even with the hardest people, and this has made a subtle but significant difference.

What I found so attractive within the discipline of Zen was a combination of two things. The quality of 'sitting quietly doing nothing' and the quality of stripping away, which is such an antithesis to how we're brought up. Together these speak to me of unlearning, of just being. There is something immensely powerful here, and it's such a contrast to how I previously lived. I feel I can explore this for the rest of my life.

In this letting go, this nakedness, there's an enormous sense of being unburdened. I've heard the Dalai Lama comment on how tough Westerners are on themselves and how self-critical we are, but in this place, all of that just drops away.

Zen master Bankei calls this place the Unborn, and it's so breathtakingly simple. It has the simplicity of a child slipping out of the classroom to a secret little den, where you can just be you, regardless of all the challenges and exams. It feels to me like complete sanity. This world can drive you crazy if you let it, but this stripping away directly resolves the relationship between me and the world, life and death, all the big questions.

I trained to teach Zen meditation and mindfulness with Daizan Rōshi, and I've found the teaching very rewarding. When you're teaching, there's no hiding. If you want to be a good teacher, you have to be authentic. Teaching is visceral and at the same time playful. So much of it happens in your interaction with others. It's a very creative process and for me a wonderful contrast to my professional life.

I'm particularly interested in teaching this work because I believe the development of this kind of awareness on the individual level can allow a deepening of relationships between humans. This, in turn, helps to bring communities together and build bridges between communities, and thus helps to establish a truly healthy society. So I'm doing this for me, for my family, and hopefully for the world.

RUTH POPLE: 'I KNOW WHO I AM'

I was introduced to meditation by my Zen yoga teacher, Dan Hozan Foxley. I was in my mid-twenties and finishing off a Master's degree. I started to practise daily for about 20 minutes or so, and then he encouraged me to go on a retreat. By this point I'd only been at it for a month or so. Here's my account of the retreat.

Who am I? Whoever thought such a simple question could be so perplexing?

Day 1
Sanzen [interview with the teacher]

'So, what arises when you pose the question, "Who am I?"'

'Well, I am these adjectives and those adjectives. I'm this noun and that noun.'

'Okay. Now, if we just put these things down here, what arises when you pose the question, "Who am I?"'

'Hmmm.'

Day 2
Sanzen

'So?'

'I'm angry. And weak. And impatient. And I feel like a fraud chanting and bowing when I don't understand why. And my knee HURTS!'

'Just keep asking the question.'

Sometime later...EUREKA!

Sanzen

'I'm nobody and everybody simultaneously. I'm no better or worse than anyone else. I have the same human needs, fears, desires. That's it, right?'

'Very good. Now if we just put that answer down here. What arises when you pose the question, "Who am I?"'

'Frustration. I was sure I'd found an eloquent, succinct [evasive] answer!'

Day 3
Sanzen

'AAARGH! I HATE this! My knees hurt, I'm tired, I'm hungry, I'm cold. I've been asking and asking just like you said and I still don't know who I am. I'll never know who I am.' [tears]

'You're doing very well.' [I'm not]

'May I ask who you are?'

'You may.'

'But you won't tell me?'

'Why don't I show you?'

I looked into Daizan's eyes and finally understood why people say they are a window into the soul. They were at once shining yet dark, dazzling yet soothing. I wished my eyes looked like that.

'I don't think I'll know who you are until I know who I am...' [more tears]

'Hmmmmm... Well, how about finding out?'

It was during breakfast that I began to feel something happening. An incredible peace had descended over me. I felt still and calm. Food felt alien on my tongue. I hadn't asked the question for a long time.

I took a shower and afterwards looked in the mirror, into my own eyes; they were dark, shiny, limitless – just like Daizan Rōshi's. During *zazen* that morning I felt an incredible energy beginning to boil inside me. Anxious not to allow it to dissipate, I avoided all other people, marching fiercely around the garden, down the lane to an old church. I stood beneath an enormous yew tree, and felt its timeless energy and calm flowing through my body. The fire inside me continued to burn, growing more and more intense.

Our Zen yoga session in the afternoon allowed me to concentrate on this feeling of power – I asked the question: 'Who am I?' Suddenly, blink! I got it, I realised. 'I know who I am.' Throughout the afternoon I continued to pose the question; each time the answer was the same. By this point I was feeling rather strange. Shivers kept running up and down my spine; I was sweating; my pupils were dilated. I couldn't keep still. Each time I inhaled I felt a rush of golden, ecstatic energy course through my body. I pressed my hot palms to my head, my heart, my knees, soothing the aches and invigorating every cell. I have never experienced anything like this pure, unadulterated joy before.

Day 4

No come-down! I am brimming with happiness and warmth towards my fellow travellers. I have tucked my discovery safely away, deep inside my belly; I know that each time I pose the question 'Who am I?' the true answer will be there waiting for me.

Going home after the retreat, I don't think my parents had ever seen me so ecstatic. I felt reborn. Over the month following the retreat, I had several more understandings where things fell into place. My understanding of myself and life has changed more than I can put into words, and I will always have that.

Of course, the high wears off as you get back into daily life, but almost on a daily basis I find little shifts still happening, even now, two years later.

After the retreat I built up to about an hour's Zen meditation every day, and it's given me a discipline and an inner strength, and I don't know how else you'd find that.

In establishing the stronger meditation practice, I've really been struck by the teachings of seeing how you really are both good and bad. Before I did this I thought I was always at least 95 per cent right, and now I'm seeing that it's not at all like that. I'm much more aware of how I can be as mean and bad-tempered as the next person, but the only sensible reaction is to change and not beat myself up.

I find I have more empathy and much less self-centredness. My ability to listen to someone else rather than just wait for my turn to talk about myself has gone through the roof. Before I did this I was incredibly judgemental, but now not so much.

I can see similarities in myself, and that means I can judge the deed rather than the person.

I now believe that if everybody did this practice, the world would be a much better place to live in. It probably sounds whimsical, but that's what my experience tells me.

SEAN COLLINS: 'I GOT IT! I UNDERSTOOD MYSELF'

My introduction to mindfulness and meditation came before my connection to Zen.

I became interested in meditation when my doctor said I was suffering from stress. At the time I was feeling very depressed. I was keen to try and do something to help myself. My partner bought me a book about mindfulness and how it can help in depression, and that book got me started in the practice.

I did an eight-week mindfulness-based stress reduction course and, after just a couple of weeks of practice, my thought patterns and suffering changed, and I was able to get myself better.

I work in a big corporate environment. Some time later I was invited to give some introductory meditation and mindfulness sessions at work. There was a lot of interest from other people also suffering from stress and pressure.

The level of interest made me keen to learn more about mindfulness and do a teacher training course, so I could teach more formally. I explored many potential training solutions and found the Zenways website, where I began to understand the history, lineage and sources of these practices.

I realised there was much more to these practices than just stress relief. I had already gained massive benefit, but the Zenways approach had so much more depth. I felt inspired to keep going myself and to try to find a way to share that with other people.

A key threshold for me was entering the Unborn (*fusho*) practice of master Bankei. The very first time Daizan Rōshi introduced it, I felt 'Wow! There's a whole other peaceful world of sensation and understanding and being that is available.' Since then I loved the Unborn meditation.

However, on an intensive Zen retreat with Daizan Rōshi I focused on the *koan*, 'Who am I?' My sister had come with me. She wasn't very experienced and this was, in the true and traditional sense, an intensive retreat. I found it challenging and I was worried that she would too.

We were in silence the whole time. I could see she was finding it tough. After a while I realised I wasn't fully focused on my practice because of my concerns for her, so I consciously attempted to just try and be 100 per cent present. To my amazement suddenly things completely shifted and changed.

I got it! I understood myself. It was not something new. It was something I'd always known, but had put out of my mind. For me it was a subtle shift but it was distinct. My perception of what's all around me became very different. Things seemed more reliable, more honest, somehow. What changed? Nothing really, just the way I saw things. Yet I felt fantastic.

In the time since this shift I've noticed a greater tolerance for people and situations, and a willingness to accept. I don't mean I don't care. I care very much. But also now it doesn't really matter what is happening. I've found that whether I'm sitting down to a beautiful meal or unblocking a drain, with the right approach, both can be very rewarding.

Previously I would do my mindfulness practice like I was taking an aspirin. I was doing it because it was good for me. Now I'm not trying to get something out of it. This is now my life! When I can see and feel all of what's going on around without the judgement and attachment, then everything is lifted, everything is positive and this has been fantastic! There's still work to do. I can see that it hasn't yet touched every area of my life. I've learned that it's not always steady upward progress. Sometimes it feels like there's a period of incubation where you're stuck, but I realise that this is part of it too, and I just need to keep going.

One of the great privileges I have gained from doing the Zenways teacher training is that I now teach the wellbeing aspect of the course in my work environment. One of the points I try to get across is: if you were a painter who turned up to a job without any paint, or a welder who came without any welding rods, it just wouldn't be good enough.

But particularly if they're having a bit of a tough time, many people show up to work with their mind elsewhere. I believe that any task you are doing, whether work-related or something at home or just speaking with someone, you'll do it better if you're paying attention! I always mention to my students that practice goes beyond your sitting place. I bring the Zen meditation and mindfulness into the day in what I call mindful moments. I've counted about 30 or 40 mindful moments each day while I work.

For example, if I have to walk to the photocopier, there are two ways I can do it: I can walk thinking, 'Oh my goodness, when is this thing going to print out? How am I going to sort this out? And then I've got to send it to somebody.' Or I can walk to the photocopier and, as I do so, simply pay attention to what's going on in the moment. Either way, it takes exactly the same amount of time to get the photocopying done. But doing it the second way I'm not in stress and, when I get back to my desk, my mind's pretty clear and I'm able to pay attention to the next thing.

I like the old analogy of the woodsman who's chopping down trees all day. He's so busy that he doesn't have time to stop and sharpen his axe. So he's working away all day long with a blunt axe. For me, meditation in the moment or mindfulness practice is about finding the mental space to come to your senses, arriving in the present moment. For me, this is just like sharpening your axe. Then when you approach the next tree, you are in the best position to deal with it.

I've found making your work the object of your mindfulness practice really boosts your work output. It takes a bit of practice to get into it, but so does everything, and, once you learn it, once you've learned how to sharpen the axe, there's definitely an improved ability to do tasks.

I don't feel like there is an end to how refined this can become. You wouldn't learn a musical instrument and at the point you get to grade one say, 'I can play this instrument and someone has told me I can play, so I'll stop now.' There is grade two that you can go on to and then grade three. My practice has exactly this feel.

I really enjoy working on improving this in my own life. And I relish the opportunity to pass on my experiences to others and enable them to get their own experiences. I particularly appreciate sharing this work in the business environment.

Also, as time goes by, I find myself recognising that I owe an acknowledgement or a debt of gratitude to the whole historic lineage that has kept this practice and this way open for us. So part of what I do is supporting this continuum as much as I can. I want to give something back, not just giving to the recipients of my courses, but also to give something back to the tradition that has come to me and needs to be kept alive for the future. So that's where my intention is – in the present, but more and more also encompassing the future and the past.

BORIS MOTIK: 'SO MUCH FEAR DROPPED AWAY AND I FELT EUPHORIC'

As a little kid in Croatia, I wasn't good at running, jumping, physical things. I would always much rather be with older people. When I was nine months old my parents had a very serious car crash. I was separated from my mother for a time; I don't know whether this was the cause, but from the age of two until I went to school, I suffered tremendous separation anxiety from my mother. And then at seven years old I had a terrible shock when I realised that I'm mortal. My parents were both atheist and my path to becoming a scientist was my feeling that this was a rational way to get control and make sense out of life.

Education went well for me. For my parents, being stupid was the worst crime that you could commit. On the other hand, they placed no value on emotions. To gain my parents' approval the only way was to excel at school, and so I did. I never really got on with schoolmates and avoided bullying by not drawing attention to myself. And then, in the seventh grade, I realised I was gay and that was even more isolating. I handled it by staying at home and studying harder.

Once I got to university I made friends with other geeks, but there was always this question of, 'Boris, why aren't you interested in girls?' Still it took me a long time to come out. I had my first sexual contact with a man only when I was 37 years old. The only reason I dealt with this was that incredible loneliness. I was single while studying at a research institute in Germany, and also when I came over to the University of Manchester. When I began working at the University of Oxford, I became professor of computer science – my dream job. My career was on the way up. Nevertheless, one day I hit the bottom. I realised if my isolation went on like this for another year I would blow my brains out.

Fortunately I was on a project that had me in Barcelona for three months, and that's when things began to change. There was a gay man in my company. It was also a common sight to see openly gay people in the street. By the time I was back in Oxford I was ready to meet someone. I got into a three-year relationship with a very nice person. This was wonderful, but it also allowed me to see all my dysfunctions playing out. I started therapy.

The process of therapy made me realise I was absolutely riddled with anxiety. I knew I couldn't carry on like this. I read a book about mindfulness and began to practise meditation and I immediately felt some relief. The realisation that it's fine to simply feel what you feel and that you can allow yourself to experience emotions without trying to wish them away was incredibly powerful.

I encountered Zenways meditation and mindfulness practices at the university and quite soon met Daizan. It was immediately obvious that this meditation stuff had tremendous potential to change lives. My response was initially to feel a lack of self-worth, to feel that this was one more field I had to try to excel at. It took a long time before I got to realising I could just be me.

On the other hand, I immediately felt quite a lot of physical benefit from meditation. I'd had a problem with severe stomach cramps. One time I began to meditate and I told myself it was fine to experience this pain without wishing it to go. After about ten minutes the pain dissipated completely for the rest of the day.

I was very ambivalent about the forms of the Zen practice – the incense, the gongs, the strange people. It felt foreign to my atheist background, but at the same time, I felt challenged by it – a challenge I had to respond to. So I was feeling my way forward with this and signed up for a Zen retreat with Daizan. It was hell. Three days of pure anxiety. It showed me that I'd had this level of anxiety underlying my life and now there was no avoiding it. I also saw how much judgement I had. I felt resentment towards people I saw as doing better than me. The whole thing was just so uncomfortable. Nevertheless, it was clear to me that this was what I needed. I saw that I couldn't live with this level of anxiety in my life underlying everything. I faced it and it started to shift.

I realised that I needed to pursue this more, and signed up for another retreat with Daizan. One thing that was tremendously helpful was reading a book called *The Self-Illusion: Why There Is No 'You' Inside Your Head*, by Bruce Hood. The book outlined psychological research showing that we're not a fixed entity with a centralised control point, but are actually much more malleable and changeable than we seem. I saw how the little intimations I was starting to get through my practice were actually squarely in line with science. On my second retreat this dimension came into sharp focus. It became vividly clear to me how everything is relative, how we use one word to define another word, that reality is not in this world of words, that there is actually nothing we need to know. It's hard to explain, but so much fear dropped away and I felt euphoric. Since then I've been able to face the future much more freely.

This sense that there's nothing to know has continued to deepen. A couple of months ago I saw how my mind constantly tries to analyse and dissect things and thus gain a sense of control. In science we try to do this, and it's clear to me how this project is useful, but through that route we will never get to the bottom of things because you're always looking at things from the outside. And the deeper you go, the more the ground you are standing on starts to shift. Some of the scientists I speak to consider the big bang to be the basis on which everything stands, but it's clearly not. So from that point onwards the sense grew that while it's okay to try to understand things, this is no way to deal with your fears, feel safe and conquer life.

Instead, I've found that life happens and all you can do is be it. One thing I discovered in meditation is how much I have this drive to escape what's happening around me – to be the safe observer who is not actually committed to the moment, who has no responsibility.

I've found a strong connection between my relationship to my body and my relationship to life in general. I now know what people mean when they talk about 'energy' in the body and in the world. For me the antidote to my sense of separation is embodiment. In meditation, when I bring myself back to my body and don't separate from whatever is arising, actually everything is fine. I'm gradually bringing this full involvement into my life, my relationships and my work. Whether what's happening is 'good' or 'bad', my role is simply to show up and not try to escape.

DIANA TRELEAVEN: 'SWIMMING IN AN OCEAN OF BLISS'

Growing up was tough for me and I had to grow up quite quickly. Residues from this tough time hung around for ages.

For a while I had a very stressful, competitive sales job. I started suffering with migraines and I kept getting a lot of infections and digestive problems. I married young. We're still together and have two lovely boys.

I developed spinal problems when I was having our first son. I was in a lot of pain. During this time ongoing emotional stuff from my past came up more and more. During the pregnancy I had a bulging disc. Over the years I developed several more. I managed it all by being very positive.

And then we had our youngest. I was very ill when I had him. Partly it was stress-related. I developed whooping cough and then severe bronchitis. On top of this was the ongoing back pain.

Our youngest son was born with multiple severe allergies, which compounded the stress and anxiety. Caring for him led me to start studying complementary health and nutrition. I started looking at different approaches and trained in reflexology and Reiki, both of which helped me with my own health issues. And I developed an interest in meditation.

I began working then as a reflexologist and I loved it. But I already had a lot of neck and spinal problems, and the pain moved into my shoulder in a big way. Just as my reflexology practice began really taking off, I started to lose the use of my right hand and arm. The doctor decided I'd got a shoulder impingement and I went in for what was supposed to be a very simple keyhole surgery operation. Afterwards the surgeon told me it looked like I'd had been in an accident. The collarbone and shoulder were forced into the soft tissue, and there was a lot of diseased bone. It was all a bit of a mystery.

The pain was even getting worse and I wasn't recovering well. I couldn't even manage the physio. I started to develop a frozen shoulder and the consultant decided that they needed to take off the end of the collarbone. So I had more shoulder surgery. By this time I'd lost the use of my shoulder and arm, and the pain was spreading to the whole right side of my body, even down into my toes, and although I didn't want to admit it, I was suffering with depression.

Finally I went to see another surgeon and they were able to get to the bottom of it all. They discovered that I had an extra rib in my neck, which was quite large and at a very awkward angle. It was compromising all the main arteries and nerves on the right side. I had a lot of years of damage to the tissues by that point. Everything was in the wrong place, and because I had severe nerve impairment, initially the surgeon didn't want to operate. There was a high risk of paralysis and a low chance of a full recovery.

I was meditating every day by this point. I could just about manage daily walking meditation on the farmland opposite our house.

I'd always been a very positive person, and this positivity helped me to keep going despite the pain. But the meditation brought me to my real turning point. I finally allowed myself to really face what was going on, to really feel terrible. For the first time in all those years I really allowed it.

I locked myself in a room, and cried and cried all day, and allowed myself to be swamped with all the feelings that came up. I just let it happen. My husband was very worried about me. I think he nearly called the men in white coats. I knew if I hadn't locked myself away, he would have wanted to rescue me. So I just sat tight. But during that day something shifted. I knew from then on that it was going to be fine, that there is all so much more than just this pain. Everything's fine. I just knew it. I opted to go for the operation on my neck despite the risks.

The operation was complicated. They had to collapse my lung and there were some tense moments, but it was pronounced a success, and I'm very grateful to the surgeon. I've been slowly recovering ever since. Despite all the drugs they've tried to give me, I deal with the pain through meditation and Reiki alone.

A couple of years after the operation I started to practise Reiki again. I found that after the treatments I tended to suggest to clients, 'You might benefit from some meditation – this can be really helpful.' Very naturally I began passing on meditation tips and I thought, 'Really, I ought to train in this.'

I started looking into courses, and I liked the look of the Zenways course, but worried whether I'd manage it physically. The course had a retreat-type setting. There was plenty of theory, but also a lot of practice. I had one day when I was awash with emotion, a lot of it to do with physical pain. I still didn't have enough grip in my hand to use a pen for long, and so I had to record the classes on a Dictaphone. Daizan told me it was fine to lie down for the meditation practice, but I was determined to sit through it like the others. My spine wasn't really strong enough to hold myself upright. The pain was too severe.

Finally I realised I had to just face the pain. I began to lie down for the meditation. All that day I was just overwhelmed with waves of emotion. But by supper time I felt washed through. I felt like a new person.

By the end of the course I felt that Zen practice was something I was living and breathing. I went home and began teaching this work. I was amazed to find I had forgiven a great deal of things from my past and was able to restore some relationships. I remember thinking, 'I feel I can cope with my life well now, I don't really think I want to be enlightened. I don't think that's what I'm here for.' I felt like I had this fantastic Teflon coating. You could throw anything at me and it slid right off.

However, I decided to go on an intensive Zen retreat with Daizan Rōshi, hoping for an extra layer of this Teflon coating.

The information on the website said: 'This retreat will be focused on *kensho*, the breakthrough experience of Zen. When you find out who you really are, your life moves on to an entirely different level.'

'Sounds good,' I thought, but didn't really believe it. I booked myself in, expecting an intensive silent retreat to help deepen my meditation practice. I had no great expectations but knew I would be in safe hands.

I certainly wasn't expecting what followed...

Day 1

Daizan explained the journey we were embarking on, and the intensive process we would be using. After just the first evening of group *sanzen*, working with the *koan* 'Who am I?', so much stuff came up that I was beginning to think, 'I'm really not sure I can do this.'

The answers came: the labels, the nouns, the roles, plus a lot of emotion attached to them. I was also beginning to feel very responsible for inviting my husband along: how was he coping? We were in silence, so, having committed myself to the process, I couldn't really ask him.

Day 2

I came into our first practice period in the morning, having had little sleep as I found the question haunted me all night long. The day continued with thoughts and feelings of: 'I can't do this.' Sadness, grief, regret, frustration, pain (physical, emotional, mental), a kind of plateau of contentment, then fatigue, exhaustion. Oh, and did I say PAIN and FRUSTRATION? I remember at this point saying: 'I'm beginning to think this process is just some crazy form of Japanese torture!'

Then, in the last period of the evening, giggles creeping in. 'I don't care who I am... I'm not sure I even want to be enlightened...just want a bit of peace...my head has had enough... don't care about the question any more... I'm just gonna switch my mind off...go to sleep...so exhausted...hurting...leave it to my subconscious to wake me up...when it's found it.' Chuckle, chuckle... More chuckling... I was letting go of the need to know... Aware of more laughter and amusement bubbling up. The bell went, indicating the end of group practice.

As I started to make my way across the room Daizan Rōshi came towards me. We sat down. I seem to remember he said: 'You're doing well...just stay with it...stay with it.'

Following this I'm just aware of the lightness of the humour building inside of me as I walked out of the meditation hall making my way towards my bed.

Then strange little chuckling noises bubbling up and coming out of me, as the KNOWING appeared, each time it came getting stronger and stronger, until I couldn't stop laughing...at the simplicity of it...so simple...laughing, smiling... It was right under my nose all the time...absurdly simple...why so difficult? ...more laughter, more involuntary bursts of laughter while trying to get to sleep...feeling so light...amazing...finally sleep.

Day 3

I woke early feeling alert and more alive than I've ever felt, the knowing still there, the question just rolling over and over all by itself, the knowing getting stronger, almost taking over my very being.

I couldn't stop smiling, feeling amazing. I checked in with Daizan Rōshi, able to tell him what I KNEW. He said: 'Well done. Enjoy it', and asked me to stay with the process, said it will help everyone. So I continued with it. The rest of the day seemed to fly by. Each time I asked the question, the knowing getting stronger, and for a good 24 hours I felt no thoughts could penetrate this.

Daizan Rōshi asked me about the times when life hadn't been so good, and although I was aware I've been through traumas, grief, sadness, difficulties, etc., in my life, I found it impossible to feel any of them. With this knowing, all these stories had come crumbling down. Peace. Letting it all go. Just present. Being. Smiling.

Day 4
Waking early again, keen to get to the meditation hall. Some thoughts had crept in: 'How would it be when I got home to my everyday life?' It was like my mind was trying to trick me, by starting to bring back thoughts. Daizan Rōshi reassured me not to worry. The morning went far too quickly. When asking the question, the same replies came over and over. I was swimming in an ocean of bliss.

And then I came on a second intensive Zen retreat working on the *koan* 'What is life?' I almost felt like I knew too quickly. I simply KNEW. And, like the first time, the knowing came with humour and laughter. It was like bubbles coming out of me, a bubbling up of laughter. It felt ridiculous; I just had to let go of the tiny knot of doubt that said I'd been deluding myself.

Since that retreat the healing's going even better and I cope really well with the physical pain. I continue my daily meditation practice and with the great joy of sharing this work with others. I've noticed that now, when stuff comes up, I deal with it in the moment and don't take it on.

Recently I had a wave of grief come up, when I was in the middle of a department store. I was suddenly awash.

Before, I would have pulled myself together and held it all in. This time I simply made my way through the store, allowed it to come as I walked away, and, by the time I'd got back to the car, it had gone. I'd let it come and I'd let it go.

I think that what I've really learned is that by fully allowing what is here to be present, I can then let go of it. My big wake-up call was getting to the point where my body almost completely stopped me from doing anything. I'd always coped with it by fighting, being strong. I would try to visualise health but it wasn't until I really allowed myself to fully acknowledge how bad it all was and coming face-to-face with both the physical and emotional pain that I really began to heal. Since that day, I haven't looked back.

Having introduced you to this selection of people, I want to re-emphasise that your journey is unique to you. As you do your practice day after day, the outlines of your own process will begin to unfold in your meditation diary.

Nevertheless, I think it's clear to see that, in each of the accounts, there's a process at work. We human beings are goal-directed animals, and I think it's helpful to have a clear intention when we engage in practice. However, when we look backwards, we tend to see the entire journey as a waking up. The breakthrough moments become just that – simply moments. It's notable that not a single one of these people thinks of themselves as finished, as fully enlightened or anything of the sort. As long as life goes on, so does the journey.

CHAPTER 12

JOINING THE LINEAGE

As I've emphasised, no one can do the practice for you. Sometimes the spiritual journey can seem a solitary one. As I put together the last chapter I was hoping it would give you a sense of others walking the path too. We become like the people we spend time with, so even more nourishing than reading about others is to actually make connections. If you can even find one or two friends to practise with you occasionally, you'll benefit tremendously.

You may find that, as you walk on, you see the world with new eyes. This new clarity can sometimes be disillusioning, but after all, disillusionment is exactly what we are seeking in genuine spiritual practice. When we let go of our illusions, we approach reality. In taking the great risk that reality is worse than our dreams, we come to the wondrous realisation that it is bigger, better and far more glorious than any dream could be.

The technical Buddhist term for this shift is *gotrabu nana*, which translates as 'change of lineage insight'. As we let go of the stuckness, the tightness, we slip into a new reality. We 'enter the stream', as the Buddha put it. In doing this we join the lineage or family of the noble ones. The Buddha was adamant that nobility wasn't an accident of birth or conferred by rituals, but was open to all, dependent on insight.

The very first time the Buddha sat down to teach, 'the spotless, immaculate vision of the Dhamma arose in the Venerable Kondanna... Then the Blessed One exclaimed: "Kondanna knows, Kondanna knows!"'[1]

This acknowledgement is referred to in Zen as: 'A thief recognises a thief.'

Will you let go into this sparkling stream and take your place in the lineage? As you do, you, too, become able to recognise others who have done so.

The Zen traditions have repeatedly attempted to institutionalise the lineage, giving it the context of temple inheritance or priestly initiation, restricting entry to (almost always male) monastics, and creating lines of succession back to the Buddha. Modern historians have demolished these fictive lineages. The true stream rolls on regardless.

Some of the greatest figures of Zen have never joined these lineages on an administrative level. When Zen master Rinzai's teacher attempted to present him with mementos of his own teacher as evidence of 'transmission', Rinzai's response was the following: 'Bring me fire.' Master Ikkyu (1394–1481) tore up his lineage certificate. Master Hakuin never received one in the first place. All of these teachers had already entered the lineage of the noble ones and gave their lives to helping others to do the same. You, too, if you keep going, will enter the stream and enjoy it fully.

And as long as one stream entrant remains in the world, the noble lineage of awakening continues.

This stream isn't far away. For all of us, our *dojo* or training ground is right where we are, in this moment. Zen Master Hakuin used an image of a lotus flower blooming in the fire.

---

1   Nanamoli, B. (1972) *Life of the Buddha.* Kandy: Buddhist Publications Society, p.45.

We don't find the truth of Zen by running away and hiding from life; we find it here, right in the middle of the fire, the stress and the pain. All the teaching you need is right here, in this moment.

And part of being in this moment is making choices. In life there are certain inescapable situations and commitments to people that have to be honoured. Change is inevitable, but we don't have to seek out some projected ideal practice place. Hakuin's most enlightened student, Satsume, came to him as a 16-year-old girl from the village. She married, had children and grandchildren, and made her ordinary life utterly magnificent. Together with our responsibilities, we modern people (somewhat paradoxically) have an extraordinary range of choice and freedom – perhaps more than human beings have ever had before.

So the question arises of how we use this choice in the context of our practice. The Zen precepts provide ethical guidance. Throughout Zen practice there is a deepening exploration of the role of right action in the world. The first public commitment to practice involves taking the precepts, and almost at the end of the *koan* study curriculum, we again challenge our understanding of these precepts. The seemingly simple injunctions not to kill, steal and so on are examined as *koans* – as spiritual questions that embody reality itself.

Some of the best advice on skilful living I have come across was given by university teacher and theologian Howard Thurman (1899–1981), who, in giving a speech, once said, 'Don't ask what the world needs, ask what is going to allow you to become truly alive, because what the world needs is people who have come alive.'

Do your very best to choose those things in life that are compelling and sufficiently fascinating for you to completely immerse yourself. When you can let go into whatever you are doing, you come alive in the process. And when you do this, you show other people what is possible and you offer a tremendous gift.

By living your life in this way, the difference that makes all the difference is your actual engagement. If you drift through life, you may learn the odd thing. But if you fully engage with all that is around you, then every hour and every moment brings you closer to your mastery of Zen.

Shinzan Rōshi often says, 'Make every day a *sesshin*.' *Sesshin* is an intensive Zen retreat, and in saying this, he is urging us to bring the commitment, vibrancy and energy that we would apply in a *sesshin* to whatever we are doing right now. He wants you to live wholeheartedly.

If you practise like this, you may well encounter incredible insights about who you are and why your life has taken the shape it has. But death and life remain mysterious. The need for superficial explanations slips away in the face of your increasing connection with the sheer magnificence of it all. You become more able to recognise and embrace the extraordinary pain and suffering that life contains. And in that acknowledgement you find a fierce joy – a warrior joy. You know that your true centre is the centre of all things and always was.

You are at home here, just as a wave is at home in the boundless ocean. Like the energy of the wave, your life impulse is neither created nor destroyed. You never gain or lose anything, and you truly have nothing to fear.

The only thing left is to dance the beginningless, endless dance of reality, and do your humble best to help in awakening others to the reality of the dance and to the unflinching warrior attitude that allows total engagement to become total transcendence, and yet most often still appears totally ordinary.

PART III

BACKGROUND MATERIAL

CHAPTER 13

SOURCE TEXTS AND ESSENTIAL TEACHINGS

'THE BUDDHA'S TEACHING ON BREATHING' FROM *THE MAHASATIPATTHANA SUTTA* (*THE GREAT DISCOURSE ON THE FOUNDATIONS OF MINDFULNESS*)

Translation by Julian Daizan Skinner and Meijia Ling

Thus have I heard.

On one occasion the Blessed One was living amongst the Kurus, at Kammasadamma, a market town of the Kuru people.

The Blessed One addressed the *bhikkhus*[1] thus: 'This is the primary way, O *bhikkhus*, for the purification of beings, overcoming of sorrow and lamentation, for the finishing of suffering and grief, for reaching the right way, for the achievement of Nibbana,[2] namely, the Four Foundations of Mindfulness.'

---

1   A *bhikkhu* is a monastic follower of the Buddha.
2   The ending of suffering, the highest goal in Buddhism.

The Four Foundations of Mindfulness

'What are these four?

'Here, *bhikkhus*, a *bhikkhu* lives contemplating the body in the body, ardent, clearly comprehending and mindful, having removed wanting and aversion towards the world. He lives contemplating the feelings in the feelings, ardent, clearly comprehending and mindful, having removed wanting and aversion towards the world. He lives contemplating consciousness in consciousness, ardent, clearly comprehending and mindful, having removed wanting and aversion towards the world. He lives contemplating mental objects in mental objects, ardent, clearly comprehending and mindful, having removed wanting and aversion towards the world.'

Mindfulness of breathing

'And how, O *bhikkhus*, does a *bhikkhu* live contemplating the body in the body?

'Here, O *bhikkhus*, a *bhikkhu*, retired to the forest, to the foot of a tree, or to an empty house, sits down, crosses his legs, straightens his body, and arouses mindfulness in the object of meditation, namely, the breath which is in front of him.

'Mindful, he inhales, and mindful, he exhales.

'Drawing in a long breath, he knows, "I inhale lengthily"; expelling a long breath, he knows, "I exhale lengthily"; drawing in a short breath, he knows, "I inhale shortly"; expelling a short breath, he knows, "I exhale shortly."

'"Experiencing the whole body, I shall inhale," intending thus, he trains himself.

'"Experiencing the whole body, I shall exhale," intending thus, he trains himself.

'"Calming the activity of the body, I shall inhale," intending thus, he trains himself.

'"Calming the activity of the body, I shall exhale," intending thus, he trains himself.

'Just as a skilful turner or turner's apprentice, cutting a long turn, knows, "I am cutting a long turn," or making a short turn, knows, "I am making a short turn," just so the practitioner, drawing in a long breath, knows, "I inhale a long breath"; expelling a long breath, he knows, "I exhale a long breath"; drawing in a short breath, he knows, "I inhale a short breath"; expelling a short breath, he knows, "I exhale a short breath."

'He trains himself with the thought: "Experiencing the whole body, I shall inhale."

'He trains himself with the thought: "Experiencing the whole body, I shall exhale."

'He trains himself with the thought: "Calming the body I shall inhale."

'He trains himself with the thought: "Calming the body I shall exhale."

'Thus he lives contemplating the body in the body internally, or he lives contemplating the body in the body externally, or he lives contemplating the body in the body internally and externally.

'He lives observing arising in the body, or he lives observing dissolution in the body, or he lives contemplating arising and dissolution in the body.

'Or his mindfulness is established with the thought: "The body exists." In this way, sufficient for the establishment of knowledge and remembrance, and he lives independently and clings to nothing in the world.

'Thus, also, O *bhikkhus*, a *bhikkhu* lives contemplating the body in the body...'[3]

---

3   And similarly for 'feelings in the feelings', 'consciousness in consciousness' and 'mental objects in mental objects'.

Ending

'Now, if anyone develops these Four Foundations of Mindfulness in this way for seven years, one of two results can be expected: either liberating knowledge right here and now, or – if there be any remnant of clinging – non-return.

'Let alone half a month. If anyone would develop these Four Foundations of Mindfulness in this way for seven days, one of two results can be expected: either liberating knowledge right here and now, or – if there be any remnant of clinging – non-return.

'This is the primary way, O *bhikkhus*, for the purification of beings, overcoming of sorrow and lamentation, for the finishing of suffering and grief, for reaching the right way, for the achievement of Nibbana, namely, the Four Foundations of Mindfulness.'

Thus was it said, and in reference to this it was so said. Gratified, the monks delighted in the Blessed One's words.

BANKEI'S ESSENTIAL TEACHINGS

Translation by Noriko Yamasaki and Julian Daizan Skinner

When your parents gave you birth you had the Buddha-heart. There were no defilements. This Buddha-heart is definitely unborn, spiritual and radiant. In the Unborn you can understand and harmonise all things.

The evidence for this is like this. If, while everybody is looking at me and listening, a crow or swallow or something else makes a noise behind you, you will distinguish them effortlessly – that is Unborn listening. This is an example. The person in this unborn spiritual radiance returns to the Buddha-heart. If you confirm this, from now you become a living Buddha.

Being Unborn doesn't depend on your previous life. Also future Buddhahood is irrelevant. An Unborn person is an enlightened person. You don't need to have *satori* (awakening) because if you're not wandering elsewhere, you are a living Buddha. Rather than trying to become a Buddha, this is the short way to simply be a Buddha.

You people listening to me – nobody is unenlightened. But when you stand up and leave this place and go home to your children or family and something you don't like happens, you lose your Buddha-heart. Until you changed it into something else, you had the Buddha-heart, but when you hold on to even a tiny thing, you immediately become unenlightened. Everyone has intelligence but when you get upset you transform yourself into a fighting spirit or hungry ghost. Then, even if somebody offers the truth to you, you can't hear it. Even if you're in the presence of truth you don't have any sense or wisdom. Then you move from hell to hell in unlimited suffering and everything becomes harder and harder and darker and darker.

Everybody has small delusions but don't transform your Buddha-heart into deluded states. You should understand this well.

BANKEI'S RETREAT TEACHING GIVEN AT ROHATSU (ON THE ANNIVERSARY OF THE BUDDHA'S ENLIGHTENMENT)
Translation by Julian Daizan Skinner and Matt Shinkai Kane

Because everyday life itself is one's practice, to say that from today you will start making a special effort to practise is incorrect. Everyone is endowed with nothing other than the Buddha mind. Therefore, if you always live in this Unborn

Buddha mind, then when you sleep, you sleep in the Buddha mind; when you wake, you wake in the Buddha mind. Living everyday life as a Buddha, there is no time when you are not one. If you always already are a Buddha, then there is no particular trying to become a Buddha. Right now *being* a Buddha is a far superior to trying to become a Buddha.

SHINZAN RŌSHI ON THE *KOAN*

When you practise with the *koan*, Hakuin says to start with the breath: inhale, bring up the *koan*, exhale, be as big as the whole universe.

There are many many *koans* but all come back to you – who are you?

Koan study is not idle thinking. We cut off idle thinking. Don't think about the *koan*; *become* the *koan*. *Koan* study is very good for scholar-types – thinking, thinking, thinking is cut off.

I like the *koan* 'mu' – only one *mu* in the whole universe. What is this *mu*? Very important *koan* for me.

If you want *kensho*, the best way is *koan* study. *Koan* is a *kensho* machine.

If you don't have a teacher, best to stay with one *koan* – go deep, deep, deep. Same thing as working with many *koans*.

Shakyamuni Buddha had one *koan*, the *koan* of human suffering (*dukkha*). That's all he needed.

Use the *koan* to cut off idle thinking. Every problem: kids ignoring their parents, ecology, population is solved if we can cut off. In English you don't have a good translation for *nari-kiru*. This is the key word in Zen. *Nari* means 'become' – become the *koan*, no gap, nothing separate. *Kiru* means 'complete' – completely cut off idle thinking.

As you develop, your *koan* study will change, you will find your own way. I don't mind what you do, just bring me a good understanding, not theories or intellectual stuff. If you can do that, on the cushion, you do what you like.

Some people say you don't need the *koan*, but show me a good Zen master these days who didn't practise with the *koan* – I haven't seen one.

Put the *koan* in your *hara* – grow, grow, grow like a mama grows a child. Soon a new baby comes.

Even Bankei Zenji started with a question, a *koan* – 'What is bright virtue?' Later he didn't need, but first he worked very, very hard. The most important *koan* is, 'Who am I?' Everything comes from that.

Why do we have many *koans*? We have to come back again and again – get the truth then throw it away many times. That we, we pile up, pile up understanding.

When sweeping, who sweeps? When weeding, who weeds? Practise like this, not just *zazen* – sitting Zen, but also *do-zen* – moving Zen or Zen in action. Make every day a *sesshin*.

NIGHT BOAT CONVERSATION
BY HAKUIN ZENJI[4]
Translation by Akane Moindron and Julian Daizan Skinner

In the spring of the seventh year of Horeki (1757), a man named Ogawa, proprietor of a bookstore in Kyoto, sent a letter to Master Hakuin's attendants at Shoinji Temple. He wrote the following:

> I have heard that the venerable teacher has a manuscript called 'Yasenkana' which describes the divine elixir of

---

4   Here Hakuin writes under the pseudonym of 'Hunger and Cold', the master of poverty hermitage.

life and the secrets of achieving longevity by training the spirit, nourishing the essence and improving the blood circulation. Seekers would value such a work considering it moisture in a drought. I've heard that parts have been privately transcribed by Zen monks. I believe keeping such a book secretly locked away is like locking away the sources of rain. Therefore, I would like to quench the people's thirst and bring healing to them by publishing this book. I know that your venerable master always enjoys serving the people. How could he begrudge us such a helpful work?

When the content of the letter was passed on by his students, the old master smiled.

Thereupon, the students withdrew the manuscript from the chest containing papers, but half of it had been eaten by moths. They worked together to amend and copy the text, which soon became 50 pages long. Finally it was ready to be sent to Kyoto. I was asked to write the preface because I happened to be senior among the students.

It has been almost 40 years since our old reverend Hakuin came to Shoinji Temple. Since then, there have been many Zen students coming to endure the severe training for even 10 or 20 years. Never thinking to flee, they were even willing to end up becoming dust beneath the temple pines. All of them were superior practitioners, courageous spiritual heroes.

For miles around the temple, the monks lived in ruins or in decaying temples and shrines. Starving in the daytime and freezing at night, they passed their days eating leaves and bran, yelled at and struck by the master. People who saw them furrowed their brows; those who heard about them sweated with fear. I'm sure even demons and monsters would shed tears and put their palms together to pray for them if they saw their situation. When they first came here, they all looked attractive and healthy, but before long they all lost weight to the point where they were worn down with exhausted facial expressions. If it were not for their brave and strong aspiration to search for the true self, what motive would there be to stay in such a place?

Due to over-zealous training, some of these monks developed lung problems and suffered from hard-to-cure diseases such as colic and pain in their loins. The old master was extremely concerned about their suffering, lowered his gaze and poured out the mother's milk of compassion by sharing the secrets of *naikan*[5] practice.

He said, 'During Zen training, if the heart becomes over-heated, we become drained in both body and mind. The five internal organs thus fall out of harmony with each other. This is a disease that no treatment or medicine can cure. Even great doctors of the past could not cure you.

'I know a secret method for restoring the elixir to its source in the *tanden*.[6] If you practise this, you'll be surprised with its amazing effect – like the sun bursting through cloud. In order to conduct this training, you need to put aside your Zen training and have a very deep sleep. But first, lie down on your back and close your eyes without falling into sleep. Extend your legs out strongly together and draw down the energy of your body to fill the navel, the stomach, the *tanden*, the loins

---

5   *Naikan* (literally, 'inner contemplation'). Hakuin's preferred term for the practices are detailed in *Yasenkana*.
6   The energy centre about three fingers' width below the navel in the centre of the body.

and legs down to the arches of your feet. While doing this imagine the following.

'This stomach and *tanden*, loins and legs, is in truth my original face.[7] How can this original face have nostrils?

'This stomach and *tanden*, loins and legs, is in truth my original home. What news from this original home of mine?

'This stomach and *tanden*, loins and legs, is the Pure Land[8] of my own heart. How is this Pure Land adorned?

'This stomach and *tanden*, loins and legs, is the Amida[9] of myself. What does this Amida of myself preach?

'If you imagine like this over and over again, the energy of your body will fill your loins and legs, and the space below your navel will swell like a gourd and soon becomes full like an inflated leather ball. After meditating like this for a week or three weeks, the disharmony of your internal organs, the depletion of your heart and energy, and your physical exhaustion will all be completely cured. If not, you may cut off this old reverend's head.'

When the students heard this, they were all filled with joy, thanked the master and each one privately carried out this secret training and experienced marvellous results. Although there were some differences in how quickly the effects were felt, depending on the exactness of their performance of the training, more than half of the students were entirely cured and sung the praises of this practice.

---

7   Another term for 'my true nature'.
8   'Pure Land' is a place particularly suitable for realising enlightenment. Hakuin is internalising what is traditionally considered an external location.
9   Amida, the Buddha of Infinite Light, is said to come to the deathbed of a devotee to conduct them forward. Again, Hakuin is internalising what is popularly conceived of as external.

The master said, 'My friends, do not be satisfied even with the complete cure of your heart-sickness. The fuller the recovery, the more the need to advance your Zen training. The deeper your penetration of the way, the more you need to press forward.

'When I was young, I suffered from an illness which was very difficult to cure. The pain was ten times greater than any of you have suffered. It became impossible for me to move, and I used to think it would be better to be dead and rid of this skin-bag. But fortunately, I was informed of the secret *naikan* training and was cured completely like you are now. My teacher said: "This is the divine art of long life and immortality. With this, even those with lower-than-average ability can live at least up to 300 years. No one can guess how a superior man might fare." With unrestrained joy, I faithfully performed the training for about three years. My heart and body became more and more healthy. My vitality restored, I gradually grew stronger.

'Then I thought, even if I live as long as Tobosaku[10] thanks to this training, if I only let life pass by without doing anything, wouldn't it be as if I am a dull and ignorant ghost protecting a corpse? Wouldn't it be like an old raccoon dog sleeping in his hole?

'No matter how long I may live, I will die at the end. Even those great hermits like Kakko, Tekkai, Choka and Hicho[11] are no longer alive. They lived long, but died. It would be better, I thought, to aspire to Buddhahood through planting the Four Great Vows, to teach the truths of Buddhism, and to fulfil the

---

10 P'eng Tsu, the Chinese exemplar of longevity, believed to have prolonged his lifespan beyond 800 years through his mastery of vitality.

11 Taoist immortals.

truly strong and indestructible *dharma*-body, which neither arises nor ceases nor decays.

'When I came to Shoinji Temple, I was followed by two or three practitioners of ability. For the past 30 years I've practised this *naikan* training along with Zen meditation. Over this time the number of practitioners here has increased one by one to a total of about 200. To those who exhausted themselves through over-zealous training or even approached derangement through over-heating of the heart, I taught the secrets of *naikan* training. Soon they were healed and able to penetrate yet deeper in their practice.

'I am over 70 years old yet without a trace of illness. My teeth have not fallen out, my eyes and ears are clearer than ever to the point where I often forget my reading glasses. I never omit my teaching of the *dharma* twice a month. In response to requests from the regions, I have held 50 or 60 meetings of three or five hundred people, lecturing on the sutras and Zen records for 50 to 70 days. I have never missed a day. I am totally healthy in body and mind, and my energy level is superior to when I was 20 or 30 years old. I know this is all thanks to the *naikan* training.'

After listening to the old master talk, everyone bowed with tears in their eyes and asked, 'Please master Hakuin, write down the main points of this *naikan*. Write it so as to preserve it and to save future sufferers from the conditions caused by Zen training.'

The old reverend nodded with agreement. This is how the manuscript was immediately written. And what is taught in this document?

The main secret of nourishing life and achieving longevity is training the body. The main secret of training the body is to concentrate the mind in the *tanden* within the *kikai* below the navel.[12] If the mind is focused there, energy concentrates in that place. If the energy is concentrated, the elixir of life is made. When the elixir of life is made, the body becomes firm. When the body becomes firm, the life force is complete. If the life force is complete, we achieve longevity. This is the secret of the nine cycles of the elixir of the sages. It must be understood that this elixir is not external to yourself.

It is important to only concentrate on making the heart-fire descend to fill the *tanden* in the *kikai*. Dear friends, if you truly practise this main secret without neglect, you will not only cure any health problems from your Zen training and recover from spiritual exhaustion, but you will also finally find an excellent solution to your long-lasting spiritual block, and will be clapping your hands and laughing with joy. Why?

> As the moon ascends, the wall-shadow is gone. (Keng Wei, 8th century)[13]

On the 25th of the first month of spring in the seventh year of the Horei era, the master of poverty hermitage, Hunger and Cold, wrote this with incense burning and head bowed.

YASENKANA (NIGHT BOAT CONVERSATION) BY HAKUIN ZENJI
Translation by Akane Moindron and Julian Daizan Skinner

When I embarked on my spiritual quest, I established the resolve to pursue it to the end. I spent two or three years

---

12 The *tanden* within the *kikai* refers to the energy centre in the centre of the body. *Tanden* translates as 'field of elixir', *kikai* as 'ocean of energy'.
13 Quotation from a T'ang dynasty Chinese poem by Keng Wei.

training to the utmost when, one night, suddenly, everything released. Like ice, all of my doubts completely melted from the root. The primal source of all the suffering of life and death vanished like a bubble. 'Ah, the way is not far away from men,' I concluded. 'I have heard that the ancients suffered many years to realise it. These tales must be a deception.'

For months I danced with delight. Allowing my arms to fly and my feet to stamp.

But after that, as I reflected on my daily life, I observed that the spheres of activity and meditation were completely out of harmony. There was always something bothering me and getting in the way.

So I decided to throw myself back into serious practice, even at the cost of my life. I set my teeth and focused my eyes for meditation, forgoing sleep and food.

Before a month had passed, my heart over-heated and scorched my lungs. My legs felt as cold as icy snow. I constantly heard noises in the ears as if I was walking along through a river valley. My liver felt weak; I was afraid of everything. My spirit was distressed and weary. Whether sleeping or awake, I saw illusions and visions. My armpits were constantly drenched with sweat and my eyes continually filled with tears. I searched out famous doctors and Zen teachers in every part of the country, but found no relief.

At that time someone told me:

'I have heard there is a man called Hakuyushi living on the cliffs in the mountains of Shirakawa in Yamashiro. He is said to be between 180 and 240 years old. He lives in the mountains miles away from human habitation. He doesn't like to meet people and will always run away if someone approaches. No one knows if he is a sage or just a fool. The people of the villages consider him wise. It is rumoured that he was formerly a teacher of Ishikawa Jozan[14] and an expert astronomer and also skilled in medicine. To those who are polite and respectful enough when asking him, he will sometimes answer questions. And if you think over those teachings later, sometimes they are highly useful.'

After hearing this, in the first month of the seventh year of Horei, I packed for the road and left eastern Mino Province where I'd been staying in a temple.

I arrived in Kyoto, crossed over Kurodani, and soon came to the village of Shirakawa. There I deposited my bundle at a teahouse and made enquiries about the location of the hermit Hakuyushi. A villager pointed over towards a mountain river.

I trekked into the mountain following the sound of the flowing water. Soon, after several miles, I reached the source of the river. There was no path beyond. I was lost. I sat on a stone and chanted a sutra. Just then a woodcutter happened by. He pointed to a spot far away up in the cloud. There I could see a yellow patch not much more than an inch square. This little object was sometimes visible and sometimes lost from view, depending on the shifting mountain mists. I was told that this was the rush curtain that Hakuyushi had hung at the entrance of his cave.

I tucked up my robes to the waist and began to climb, stamping up the rocks and pushing the grasses aside. Icy snow

---

14 A *samurai* patron of the arts and Chinese learning whose Shisendo (Hall of the Poetry Immortals) can still be visited in the north-eastern outskirts of Kyoto. It seems that Hakuyushi was more likely Ishikawa's student than his teacher.

bit through my straw sandals and the damp mists wetted my clothes. I was sweating when at last I reached the rush curtain. The view was of exquisite purity, the place, far above, worldly dusts. My heart and soul started to tremble and my skin felt a shiver. I sat on a rock and calmed myself by counting my breath up to several hundred. I gathered all my courage, shook the dust off my robes, straightened out my collar, and hesitatingly and timidly rolled up the rush curtain.

There I was able to dimly see hermit Hakuyushi sitting up straight with his eyes closed. His white hair reached to his knees, but his face was ruddy and clear. He was draped in a rough cloth and sat on a straw mat. The cave itself was barely five or six feet square. There was absolutely nothing to eat. On a low desk were placed Confucius' *Doctrine of the Mean*, *Lao-Tzu* and *The Diamond Sutra*.[15] I made the most respectful greetings, told him the symptoms of my illness, and asked him for help.

After a while, the hermit opened his eyes and looked at me carefully. He spoke slowly: 'I'm only a useless old man withering away in the mountains. I live by gathering chestnuts for food and sleeping beside mountain deer – a complete ignoramus. I am so sorry that the time a distinguished monk would expend in hoping to meet a sage should be so wasted.'

Again and again I earnestly repeated my request for aid. Finally he took my hand to take my pulse and examine the condition of my internal organs. I noticed his nails were about 1.5cm long. He furrowed his brow and with an expression of pity said: 'The situation is serious. Your illness arises because you over-strained in your Zen meditation. A Zen sickness like this cannot be treated with medical methods. If the sages of

---

15 Key texts of the Confucian, Taoist and Buddhist traditions.

medicine gave you acupuncture, moxa and herbs, their efforts would be fruitless. Since you became ill because of *rikan*,[16] the only way left for the cure is *naikan*.[17] There is a saying: "If you fall on the ground, from the ground you must stand."'

'Please teach me the essential secrets of *naikan*,' I said. 'I will practise it along with my Zen study.'

The hermit adopted the expression and posture of solemnity and began speaking slowly. 'You are a true seeker. Well then, I will tell you a little of what I have learned in the past. This is the secret of preserving life and few know it. Diligently master this method and you will experience marvellous effects. Also your life will be extended.

'Now, the great way, the source of all things, is divided into the two principles of Yin and Yang. When these two harmoniously come together, humans and all things are created. There is an innate vitality in humans flowing through the human body. Thanks to this the internal organs function well. The energy and the blood mutually rise and fall to circulate about 50 times each day and night.

'The lungs are feminine organs embodying the metal element, and sit above the diaphragm. The liver is a male organ, the wood element, and has its seat below. The heart, the fire element, is the Sun Great Yang,[18] placed on high. The kidneys embodying the water element are great Yin, and rule below.

---

16 *Rikan*: contemplation of reality – meditation practices to realise the truth of things.

17 *Naikan*: inner contemplation – practices to strengthen, energise and re-balance the body.

18 Referring to noon when the sun is at its hottest.

In the five organs[19] there are seven sublime forces, the spleen and kidneys both having two.

'The exhalation comes out of the heart and lungs, and the inhalation enters the liver and kidneys. Each exhalation causes a movement of the blood and energy of about three inches, and with each inhalation there is a movement of the blood and energy of about three inches. There are about 13,500 full breaths during a full day and night, causing this circulation 50 times. Fire is light and therefore always goes upward, and water is heavy and therefore always flows downwards. If a person does not understand this and exceeds the appropriate measure of meditation, or thinks too much, the heart will over-heat and the lungs burn out. When the lungs that are the metal mother are over-loaded, the kidneys, the water children, are weakened. Mother and child are both damaged and the internal organs thus fall out of harmony. This causes the four elements of the body, earth, water, fire and wind, to lose their mutual balance and create innumerable illnesses. Once this happens, no treatment or physician can prevail.

'The maintenance of life may be compared to defending a country. An enlightened ruler always gives his devotion to the people, but the unenlightened ruler always pays attention to the upper classes. If the ruler only attends to the upper classes, they become too arrogant in their authority and will lose consideration for the poverty and sufferings of the people. The people then weaken, the land sees famine and death fills the streets. The virtuous and wise hide. Resentment burns amidst the masses. Local nobles isolate themselves and

---

19 The spleen, the earth element, has not been mentioned; most likely it was simply overlooked.

foment rebellion. Barbarians attack the borders. The suffering of the people reaches a peak and the country dies.

'But contrary to this, if the ruler pays his attention principally to the people, the upper classes and officials restrain their ambitions and consider always the hard labours of the people. Then the farmers produce abundant grain, the women produce abundant cloth. The virtuous and wise willingly serve the ruler. The local nobles show respect and obedience. The people become prosperous and the country strong. No one will disobey the law, no enemies threaten the frontier, and there will be no tumult of war. The people will forget weaponry.

'The human body is just like this. A man who perfectly masters the way always attends to the lower, filling the lower body with his heart energy. If the heart energy fills the lower body, the seven ills cannot operate, nor can the four evils invade. The circulation of energy and blood will be sufficient to make heart and mind vigorous. The mouth will not taste medicines, the body will not experience the distress of needle and moxa.

'But the unenlightened person does the contrary and allows their heart energy to flare upwards. The heart-fire on the left side thus scorches the lung-metal on the right. The five senses are dimmed and the six auxiliary organs fall into disharmony. The Chinese sage Shitsuen[20] thus counsels, "The true man always breathes from the heels; the ordinary man always breathes from the throat." Kyoshun[21] teaches, "When energy fills the lower body, the breath is long; when energy fills the

---

20 The great Taoist Chuang Tzu.
21 Hsu Chun, an eminent Korean master of medicine.

upper body, the breath is short." Jyoshi[22] says, "In man the energy is unified. When it descends to the lower body, that is the arising of single Yang.[23] When Yin reaches completion and returns to single Yang, the evidence is the feeling of heat in the *tanden*." The general principle for the nourishment of the health is that the upper body should always be cool and the lower body cool.

'There are 12 energy channels in the body [meridians]. The channels are 12-branched and correspond to the 12 months and the 12 hours of the day. They also relate to the six lines of each hexagram that change through 64 permutations over the course of the 12 months of the year.

'When there are five Yin lines above and one Yang line at the bottom, we call it the hexagram of "Earth thunder returns".[24] This corresponds to the winter solstice and indicates that the true man breathes with his heels.

'When there are three Yang lines at the bottom and three Yin lines on top, we call it the hexagram of "Heaven and earth in harmony"[25] and it corresponds to the season of new year. In this season, everything is filled with the energy of growth and hundreds of flowers receive the blessing of spring. This is the configuration of the true man who fills his lower body with energy. If a man achieves this, his energy and blood will be replenished and become doughty and vigorous.

---

22 Shang Yang, a Chinese doctor from the Yuan dynasty (1271–1368), considered an authority on the arts of longevity.

23 Referring to the Chinese *I Ching* (*Ekikyo*, in Japanese), *The Classic of Changes*, a divination text, the most ancient of the Chinese classics. Its comments on 64 hexagrams – combinations of six Yin and Yang lines – have been used to track the flow of change in life and situations.

24

25

'When there are five Yin lines at the bottom and one Yang line on top, we call it "mountain and earth riven"[26] and the season is autumn. In this season, trees in the forests wither and hundreds of flowers wither and fall. This expresses the ordinary man who breathes with the throat. If a man is in this condition, his body will weaken and wither and his teeth will fall out. It is said in the *Yojo-sho*,[27] "When the six Yang lines are all exhausted and become Yin, man will die."[28] Therefore you should know that the most important point in maintaining life is to fill the lower body with energy.

'In ancient times, when Tokeisho purified himself and visited Master Sekidai[29] to ask for the main secret of the elixir of life, the master said, "I possess the main secret of the elixir but it can only be told to one of great capacity. This secret is what Kokeishi transmitted to the Yellow Emperor."[30] The Emperor is said to have performed purification practices for 21 days before he received it.

'The great way is nothing other than this elixir; and this elixir is nothing other than the great way. There is a teaching called the elimination of leaking from the five sense organs. When a man abandons his six desires and each of his five sense organs forgets its function, the harmonious essential true energy will accumulate before his eyes. This is what the famous Taoist Taihaku[31] referred to when he said, "the heavenly within

---

26
27 A text on prolonging and nourishing life.
28
29 Unknown figure.
30 The legendary Yellow Emperor gives his name to the source text of Chinese medicine. A dialogue between Kuang Ch'eng and the Emperor similar to the above is found in the *Chuang Tzu*.
31 T'ai-pai Tao-jen; not known.

me united with the heaven which is its source", and what Mencius[32] referred to as "the vast flowing energy". A man needs to draw this energy down and store it in the space below the navel, in the *kikai tanden*. If he maintains this for months and years without distraction, one morning, the elixir furnace will turn over and everywhere, within and without, will become one great circulating elixir. He will realise that he himself is older than heaven and earth, deathless as space. This is true alchemy. It is not a trivial method for flying in the sky on the wind and mists, or walking on the water. The true immortal can churn the ocean into cream and transform earth into gold. A wise man amongst the ancients said, "The elixir is the place below the navel. One circulates the blood of the lungs, the liquid gold, down into the *tanden* so this golden fluid can be sublimated into the elixir.'"

After hearing this I said to the hermit, 'I have listened with awed attention to all you have said. From now, I will discontinue my Zen meditation for a while and practise this method to cure my sickness. But I have one doubt. I wonder if the method you have taught me would not over-cool my heart, which the physician Rishisai[33] warned about. Also, if I fix my mind to one place, won't it stagnate the circulation of energy and blood?'

The hermit smiled and said, 'No. Rishisai also said, "The nature of fire[34] is to burn upwards, so it must be brought downwards. In contrast, the nature of water[35] is to go down and so it must be raised upwards. When the water is

---

32 Mencius (372–289 BC), the most famous Confucian philosopher.
33 Li Shih-ts'ai, a noted Ming-dynasty Chinese doctor.
34 ☲ – the trigram entitled 'Fire'.
35 ☵ – the trigram entitled 'Water'.

brought up to the fire moving down, the meeting is called 'intercourse'. When such intercourse occurs it is said to be Fulfilment,[36] and when the intercourse doesn't occur it is said to be Unfulfilment.[37] The former is the symbol of life and the latter is the symbol of death." When Rishisai warns of over-cooling, it was to save people falling into the one-sided error of Tankei.[38] An ancient says, "When there is illness in the body, the ministerial fire, the fire of the liver and kidneys, tends to rise up. In this case one must use water to control the fire."

'There are two kinds of fire, lordly fire and ministerial fire. The lordly fire is above and rules stillness, while the ministerial fire is below and rules motion. The lordly fire is the master of the heart, and the ministerial fire is like a minister supporting him. This ministerial fire has two parts, the kidneys and liver. The liver corresponds to thunder and the kidneys correspond to the dragon. Therefore it is said, "If one returns the dragon to the bottom of the sea, there will certainly be no sudden thunder, and if one stores the thunder in the marsh, there will be no dragon flying wild. The ocean and marsh are both water." This expression indicates the means by which the fire is kept from ascending.

'It is also said that when the heart is exhausted, its energy is depleted and it over-heats. In order to restore the heart energy, one must draw it down and bring it together with the kidneys. This is called restoration, the method of fulfilment, the intercourse of water and fire. In your case, you

---

36 ☰☰ – water over fire (the cooking pot over the stove).

37 ☰☰ – fire over water: fire tending to rise up and water to sink; dissolution and separation.

38 The *Tan-his* school of medicine that presumably emphasised developing the Yin or cooling energies of the body.

developed this illness because your heart-fire has been blazing upwards; there is no other way to cure but bring this fire into the lower body.

'In addition, even though my method is similar to that of the Taoists, you should not think that this is different to Buddhism. This is Zen. One day you will realise, remember these words and smile.

'True meditation is non-meditation. False meditation is drifting and unfocused. You have been engaged in drifting meditation and developed this illness; now you should rely on the method of non-meditation. If you lower the heart-fire and place it in the *tanden* and down to the soles of your feet, your chest will naturally feel cool and there will be no discrimination or troubling illusions. This is true meditation, pure meditation.

'You said that you would drop your Zen meditation for a while, but this is not good. The Buddhist sutras say, "If you fix your attention on the soles of your feet, every illness is cured", and in the teaching of the *Agama Sutras*,[39] there is a method of contemplation which uses cream that is very effective in curing fatigue of the heart.

'In *The Great Cessation and Contemplation* of Master Tendai Chigi,[40] several Zen illnesses are described, and the cure for each is explained in extreme detail. There is a method to cure different diseases by 12 different ways of breathing, and a method to concentrate the heart and energy into the navel

---

39 *Agama Sutras*, the Chinese versions of the Buddha's earliest teachings. This contemplation method has not been discovered in these sutras, but the *Kuan Fo San Mei Hai Ching* (*Scripture on Contemplating the Ocean of Buddhas*), a later sutra, contains a markedly similar method.

40 Chigi (538–597), founder of the Chinese Tien T'ai tradition and author of this monumental work on Buddhist meditation practice.

through visualising a bean there. But the key point of all the methods is to lower the heart-fire to the place below the navel and down as far as the soles of your feet. These methods not only cure diseases, but are also very helpful in Zen meditation.

'There are two kinds of cessation, cessation in the context of true emptiness and cessation in the context of things. The former is contemplation of the true reality of all things, and the latter emphasises lowering the heart-energy in the navel – *kikai* and *tanden*. If a student practises these methods, he will certainly experience a huge effect.

'Long ago, Dogen,[41] founder of Eiheiji Temple, travelled to China and consulted with Zen master Nyojo of Tendo Mountain. Upon Dogen's entrance and prostration, Nyojo taught, "When one meditates, the attention must be placed on the palm of your left hand", and this is basically the method by which master Chigi saved the life of his dying brother. It is described in detail in *The Lesser Cessation and Contemplation*.

'Also, the master Hakuun[42] said, "I always make my heart-energy fill my abdomen. Every day I train students, meet with guests and teach, and this method is most effective to a point where I believe it becomes more effective as I get older." These true words must be based on the quotation from the Somon medical classic: "If one is peaceful, unstrained and free from greed, and the heart is kept empty, the true energy will follow. If one guards the spirit inside, illness cannot enter." The main meaning of "guarding the spirit inside" is to fill the whole body, all 360 joints and 84,000 pores, with the original energy. This is also the true way of nourishing life.

---

41 Dogen (1200–1253) received the *dharma* transmission from Chinese Zen
    master Tendo Nyojo and introduced the Soto Zen tradition to Japan.
42 Po-yun, Chinese Zen master.

'Hoso[43] says, "The method of keeping the spirit peaceful, of filling the body with energy and of calming the heart is like this: first, close the door of the room, prepare a bed, warm the sheets and have a pillow two-and-a-half inches high. Lie down there, close your eyes and hold the heart-energy in the breast. When you exhale from the nose, do it very slowly to an extent that even if you have a feather on the tip of your nose, it would not move at all. If you continue breathing like this for about 300 times, you will hear nothing and see nothing. When you reach this point, heat and cold cannot invade you; bees and scorpions cannot poison you. You will live up to 360 years old and approach the state of the true man."

'Also, poet Sotoba[44] teaches a method of *naikan* like this: "Eat when you are hungry but stop eating before you are full. Take a walk. Once your stomach is empty enter a quiet room, sit down in the correct posture and count your inhalations and exhalations. Count from one to ten; from ten to one hundred; from one hundred to one thousand. Soon your body will be still and peaceful as a rock; your heart will be calm and open as the empty sky. If you maintain this for a long time, your breathing will cease; there are neither inhalations nor exhalations. The breath will then seep out of your 84,000 pores and rise like a mist. The source of all your illnesses from unremembered times will be gone. It is like a blind person suddenly receives his sight. You no longer have to ask people the way. All you need to do is reduce talking and preserve and nourish your original energy. This is the reason why it is said, 'Always close your eyes if you want to nurture your eyes, stop listening and

---

43 P'eng Tsu, Chinese philosopher.
44 Sotoba (1037–1101), eminent Chinese poet and Zen practitioner.

close your ears if you want to nurture your ears and always remain silent if you want to nurture your heart-energy.""'

Then, when I asked, 'Would you please teach me the method of the *naikan* using soft ointment?', Hakuyushi said the following.

'If the student of Zen practice finds the condition of body and mind approaches exhaustion and the four elements fall into disharmony, it is good to gather the spirit and imagine the following.

'First of all, imagine a ball of soft healing ointment with pure colour and scent and the size of a duck's egg. Place this ball on top of your head. Experience it melting. Its delicate touch sinks through the bones and moistens and soothes the inside and outside of your head. The exquisite feeling will then sink deeper and go down to the shoulders and arms, the chest, the diaphragm, the lungs, the liver and intestines, the stomach, till at last it reaches the bottom of the spine and the buttocks. As it washes downwards like this, the disharmonies and excess energy of the internal organs accumulated in the chest, together with the pain caused by this accumulation, will all descend with a sound just like flowing water. The ointment will sink down through the whole body, warming and moistening the legs, then reach down to stop at the soles of the feet.

'Then imagine this flow, which has gone down through the body, then accumulates to warm and fill the lower body until you feel as if you are internally bathed in a decoction of fragrant herbs that have been mixed and heated together by a expert physician, warming and healing everything below the navel. Since everything is just a reflection of your mind, if you imagine like this, you will actually become aware of a rare scent, and your body will feel exquisite sensations. Body and mind will harmonise, and you will have more vitality than when you were 20 or 30 years old. Blocks and accumulations in the body dissolve. Your digestive organs will function perfectly. Before noticing it, your skin is bright and shining.

'If you continue this practice without laziness, what diseases cannot be cured? What virtue cannot be acquired? What wisdom cannot be achieved? What practice cannot be accomplished? The results simply depend on your application.

'When I was young I suffered from frequent illnesses ten times worse than you. I visited all kinds of doctors and tried hundreds of treatments only to find there was no cure. Thereupon I prayed to the deities and implored the help of the heavenly immortals until I was blessed to receive this wonderful soft ointment method. Filled with joy, I practised the method without intermission and within a month most of my diseases disappeared.

'Since then, body and mind are both in their best condition, working marvellously. From that time nothing bothers me. The year and month are not my concern. Worldly thoughts have been slowly vanishing, and human desires are gone. I have lost track of my age.

'I wandered in the mountains in Wakasu province for about 30 years. Nobody knew me. Looking back on that time, it seems like the dream of Koryan.[45] Now I live in this uninhabited mountain of Shirakawa with two or three cotton cloths on this old body, yet I never get sick, even in the hardest winter. Even when stocks of food run down, sometimes for months, I don't feel frozen or starved.

---

45 Who, during the duration of his supper cooking, dreamed a whole career of success in the administration, and as he awoke, realised the pointlessness of ambition.

'This is all thanks to the *naikan*. Now I have presented to you secrets that cannot be exhausted even over the course of the longest life. There's nothing more for me to say.'

He finished talking, closed his eyes and remained sitting in silence.

With grateful tears in my eyes, I thanked him and left the cave.

I slowly descended from the cave entrance; the sun was setting on the trees. I heard the sound of wooden clogs echoing in the mountain valley. In awe and wonder I anxiously looked around. Hakuyushi the hermit had come out of the cave to guide my way. As he approached he said, 'No one enters these mountains. There's no path, so it is easy to become lost. To spare you this trouble I will guide you down for some way.'

He was wearing high wooden clogs and carried a thin stick. He walked ahead of me down the rocky way while chatting and laughing as easily as if he was walking on a flat field. After descending a few miles, we reached the stream. The hermit said, 'Follow this stream and you will reach Shirakawa village.' He turned and went back.

I was sad to be parted from him and stood awhile following his return with my eyes. His pace was strong and swift, as if he was flying to a mountain retreat to escape from the world. I looked up at him in admiration and respect, knowing that this must be the last time I would meet and learn from such a man.

I came back to Suruga and secretly immersed myself in the *naikan* method taught by the hermit. Before three years had passed all of my former illnesses had disappeared without receiving herbs, moxa or the needle.[46] Not only was I cured, but also many difficult-to-handle, difficult-to-follow,

---

46 Methods of acupuncture.

difficult-to-understand, difficult-to-enter *koans*, which previously I could find no footing, no handhold, no place to bite, clarified, and I experienced the great joy of enlightenment at least six or seven times without counting countless small joys, my body rapturously dancing. I realised that the words of Zen master Daie,[47] who said, 'Eighteen huge enlightenments and countless small enlightenments', were actually the truth.

Previously, I used to put on two or three pairs of socks and still felt icy-cold in the soles of my feet, but now I don't wear socks or use a heater even in the middle of a severe winter. I am over 70 years old with no illnesses; this is all thanks to this *naikan*.

Now, readers, don't think that doddering old Hakuin has spewed out a mass of drivel trying to deceive good people. I did not write this for intelligent people with superior natures who can reach the goal at one stroke from the master. I want dullards like me who are suffering from severe illnesses to read it. If they study this carefully and practise the meditation, I can guarantee it will help. I only fear that others might clap their hands and laugh at me. Why?

The horse that chews the dried-up winnow disturbs the man's afternoon nap. (Huang T'ing-chien, 1045–1105)[48]

---

47 Daiye Soko (1089–1163), Sung-dynasty Chinese Zen master, one of Hakuin's major influences.

48 Line from a Chinese poem by Huang T'ing-chien, meaning superior seekers might be disturbed from their serenity by these words as the sleeper is disturbed by the horse.

FROM HAKUIN'S *ROHATSU*[49]
RETREAT INSTRUCTIONS

Translated by Matt Shinkai Kane and Julian Daizan Skinner

Prepare a thick cushion and sit in a cross-legged position. Wear your clothes loose, straighten the spine, settle the body, and begin counting the breath. This practice of counting the breath is the best way to enter into *samadhi*. At this point, fill the *hara* with energy and then bring complete focus to your *koan*. You should resolve with all of your being to maintain this concentration.

Those who continue this sole, unrelenting focus on their *koan* for a period of time will without a doubt experience *kensho*. Those who exert themselves in this way without becoming lazy will achieve it as surely as one who attempts to strike the ground does in fact do so. Therefore exert yourself! Strive on!

There are six great methods within the practice of counting the breath: counting, following, stopping, observing, returning to the source, and purification. Through counting the breath, one enters into *samadhi*; this is called *su*. When this practice ripens, simply follow the natural flow of the breath and enter into *samadhi*. This is known as 'following the breath'.

In total there are 16 excellent practices but they all boil down to two: *shi*, to count the breath, and *zui*, to follow the

---

49 December the 8th is the day Japanese Buddhists celebrate the enlightenment of the Buddha. In Zen temples the previous seven days are occupied by the most intensive retreat of the year – the *Rohatsu* retreat.

breath. Therefore the first ancestor, Bodhidharma, said, 'Let go of external things, keep the mind free from internal grasping, and, with the mind like a great wall, enter the Way.'

With the mind free from internal grasping, you ground in the source. With the mind like a great wall you progress directly forward. There is deep meaning in these words. I therefore urge you to listen deeply, make your mind like a great wall, and continue to progress in your practice! If you follow these instructions, you will achieve *kensho* even more surely than one who attempts to strike the ground does so. Exert yourself in your practice! Strive on!

CHAPTER 14

SHINZAN AND DAIZAN, TWO LIVES

SHINZAN RŌSHI[1]

When I asked Shinzan Rōshi about his life, he began by telling me indirectly why I was there talking to him. As a child in northern Japan during the closing stages of the Second World War, he and his friends were given sharpened bamboo poles by an older boy, and drilled in 'killing an American'. Day after day they practised, knowing they were rehearsing their deaths. Then suddenly the war was over. Japan had capitulated.

In no time at all friendly American soldiers had arrived and were giving the kids sweets and teaching them baseball. 'Something in me unwound,' Shinzan Rōshi said. 'I cried.' After that he was always open to Westerners, unlike many in the Japanese Zen world.

You'll find a fuller account of his life in the book *The Zen Character: Life, Art and Teachings of Zen Master Shinzan Miyamae*.[2] Here we will just cover the highlights.

---

1 Daizan's teacher and abbot of Gyokuryuji.
2 Julian Daizan Skinner (2015) *The Zen Character: Life, Art and Teachings of Zen Master Shinzan Miyamae*. London: Zenways Press.

Adjusting to post-war life, the young man had dreams of becoming a successful businessman. But two of his business ventures crashed. He lost not only all of his money, but his parents' money as well.

In complete despair he considered suicide. He even laid his head on the railway tracks but felt unable to go through with it. Everything he touched, even suicide, had turned to failure.

By chance, one day he offered an elderly Zen nun a ride from the railway station back to her temple. Her kindness and twinkling good humour awakened a new possibility. She gave him a book on Zen called *Senshin Roku* (*On Purifying the Heart*). He began to read and his life began to change.

Not long afterwards, he was ordained a Rinzai Zen monk (wearing robes sewn by the nun) by Mitsui Daishin Rōshi at Zuiryoji, a Zen training temple in Gifu, central Japan. As this temple was close to the distractions of a city centre, it tended not to attract the most dedicated Zen students.

Daishin Rōshi recognised Shinzan's sincerity, and sent him to study with his own master, the renowned Kajiura Itsugai Rōshi at Shogenji, deep in the mountains. Known as *oni sodo* (the devil's *dojo*), Shogenji had the reputation of being the strictest Zen training temple in Japan.

The new monk, Shinzan, went to Itsugai Rōshi, desperately looking for someone who had already awakened and who, in turn, could help him to awaken to something beyond his own misery. He wasn't disappointed.

Many times Itsugai told the story of how as a young Zen monk he had practised at Daitokuji Temple in Kyoto. Although he practised sincerely, the liberating insight of *kensho* was slow to come.

He vowed to meditate all night in the temple graveyard for 100 days. It was in the middle of winter, and of all Japan,

Kyoto is notable for its winter cold. Even when snow fell on him, the earnest young monk didn't falter in his practice. When he went to see his teacher for *sanzen*, sometimes Itsugai would faint from cold. He battled on through 100 days, seeming to make no progress at all.

Then came a rest day. His brother monks wandered into the city, but not Itsugai. He walked to a nearby shrine that his mother used to visit. He bowed his head and prayed that his spiritual eye would open. Then he returned to Daitokuji and continued his meditation.

Evening came; it began to get dark, but the monks had not yet returned. Their laundry was still hanging outside, so he brought it in, mindfully folded it and placed it in front of their rooms.

The rest day is also the bathing day in a Zen temple, so he prepared the bath, anticipating the return of the others. He filled the furnace with firewood. Unconsciously, automatically, he piled on more wood and lit the fire. All of a sudden a stream of fire and heat came out and hit his body. At that moment he realised his true nature. The returning monks found him dancing and singing with joy.

Itsugai was a strict teacher. At the beginning, he wouldn't even allow the new monk Shinzan to attend *sanzen*. Things only started to change when he spotted Shinzan walking back to Shogenji after a week spent meditating alone in a cave.

Even then he was considered an outsider. Shinzan was already 30 by this time and the other junior monks were in their late teens or early twenties. And it wasn't just his age that marked him out as unusual.

Shinzan encountered some wonderfully true-hearted practitioners. But many of his fellow monks came from temple priestly families. Rather than coming with the intention of seeking awakening, many of them wanted to do a certain minimum amount of *shugyo* or ascetic training in the monastery, so they could qualify as priests and go home to assist their fathers. Eventually they would become, in turn, the new priests of their temples. Being almost ten years older, with no temple connections and a burning quest to find some meaning in life, the misfit Shinzan was nicknamed *oji* (grandad).

Itsugai Rōshi gave him the traditional *koan*, or spiritual question, of *mu*. The Zen master Joshu was asked by a young monk whether a dog had a Buddha nature, to which he answered *mu* or 'No'. 'What is this *mu*?' challenged Itsugai. 'Bring me this *mu*.' While absorbed in this question, Shinzan was out on the mountain behind Shogenji one night. He shouted '*mu*', with his whole being. 'I lost myself,' he explained simply. 'After that many *koans* pass, pass, pass.' He had realised *kensho* – his true nature.

In the Rinzai approach to Zen study, the understanding is deepened and broadened through facing many *koans* in sequence. Different lineages have different programmes and also slightly different ways of dealing with this material. More *kensho* experiences followed, and Shinzan grew in confidence. As time passed it became clearer to him how, despite the sincerity of the few, many in the monastery were not there to gain spiritual insight, or even to simply support their family traditions. The big motivator was money.

Funerals were the source of cash. Big money could be made from providing them.[3] Ordinary people, feeling exploited, were losing trust in the temples. The scandal grew to the point that in the 1984 satirical film *Ososhiki*, which portrays a Japanese funeral, the Buddhist priest arrives to conduct the ceremony

---

3   A family might end up paying the equivalent of US$5000–6000.

in a white Rolls-Royce limousine.[4] Shinzan believed that the Japanese Zen system was in urgent need of restoration.

His practice continued to mature. Gradually he mastered all the hundreds of *koans* of the Mino branch of the Inzan line of Rinzai Zen, taught at Shogenji. One day Itsugai Rōshi looked intently at him. Their eyes locked. Fire met fire. Itsugai said, 'As surely as my eyes are black you are worthy to be the Zen master of Shogenji.'

Developments intervened, however. Itsugai Rōshi, believing that he could best serve others by expanding his reach, progressed from running Shogenji to become the abbot of the head temple, Myoshinji.

Itsugai Rōshi wanted Shinzan to receive his Zen master's paperwork from another senior monk. But Shinzan's feeling was that since this senior monk had not yet penetrated to genuine understanding (and Itsugai readily agreed with his assessment), the process would be meaningless.

So Shinzan moved on, making public his misgivings. Someone who hasn't reached understanding himself, Shinzan believed, cannot help others to do so any more than a blind person can help others to see. He had created a powerful enemy. 'Anyway,' Shinzan said, 'everybody already called me Rōshi, Rōshi.'

He moved into a tiny temple deep within the mountains, and began to travel to study at Kokutaiji, a prestigious training temple near Japan's north coast. After some time, Shinzan was offered the position of Zen master of Kokutaiji, following on from Inaba Shinden Rōshi.

---

4   The clip can be viewed on YouTube at www.youtube.com/watch?v=kUX3dXfDJpw

His bête noire from the past intervened behind the scenes and made the appointment impossible.

Undaunted, Shinzen Rōshi stepped out of the Rinzai Zen mainstream and restored Gyokuryuji, the abandoned hermitage of the great 17th-century Zen master Bankei. Realising that he actually had little interest in running a school for funeral priests, he put up a sign at the hermitage reading, 'Training place for young and old people to realise their true nature.'

Over the 14 years or so of my Zen monastery training I'd experienced my own share of temple politics, and I'd long come to the conclusion that while enlightened individuals are rare, enlightened organisations simply don't exist. But there was something in Shinzan Rōshi's story I didn't understand: his simultaneous celebration of the teachings of Hakuin and Bankei.

Looking into the events of Bankei's life, Shinzan Rōshi felt a great affinity with the staunch independence and boundless kindness of the former Zen master. 'Bankei helped many people,' he said. 'I wanted to do the same.' At the same time he upheld the fierce goal-directed focus of Hakuin. He took the unprecedented step of making Bankei's gentle teachings and the warrior intensity of Hakuin-style practice available simultaneously.

His journey to the margins of Zen had allowed Shinzan Rōshi to focus his teachings on what he believed to be truly important – the development of transformative spiritual insight. He frequently began his *dharma* talks with the following: 'The first priority is *kensho*; the second priority is *kensho*; the third priority is *kensho*.' Different people, Shinzan realised, would find this insight in different ways.

Moreover, Shinzan Rōshi recognised that people needed funerals, but as he was so disturbed by the modern distortions of Zen through excessive funeral fees, he began teaching laymen how to conduct them free or at low cost. There were howls of outrage from the temple priests whose income was potentially being undercut, and he was asked to desist. Shinzan refused, and after an inconclusive spat in the regional courts,[5] he parted ways with the Myoshinji branch of the Rinzai school and focused on *zaike bukkyo* (lay-based Buddhism). He is the honorary founder of Zendo Kyodan (literally, 'Zenways community'), and other *sanghas* both in and outside Japan. All of these independent Zen organisations honour the lineage of teaching that Shinzan Rōshi had received, but remain outside the financial and administrative structure that had become so problematic.

Shinzan Rōshi's fearless way of living continues to inspire controversy. He was always particularly welcoming of people outside the mainstream of society. He accepted *hikikomori* (young people who had been bullied into withdrawing to their bedrooms), retired men thrown out by their wives, and even gangsters. Sometimes I felt I was living with Jesus (although Shinzan never exuded an air of sanctity).

In recent years, probably the most hated people in Japan have been the leaders and members of the doomsday death cult, *Aum Shinrikyo*. One of the senior members, Kazuaki Okazaki, caused consternation when he was involved in the horrific murder of anti-cult lawyer Tsutsumi Sakamoto, his wife, and their infant son.

After his arrest, Okazaki underwent various psychological tests and a cult-deprogramming process. No one could get to him; he was rock-solid in his belief that what he'd done

---

5   Paradoxically, Shinzan Rōshi stood accused of profiting from his teaching of funerals – given the lie by his simple and austere lifestyle.

was right. Shinzan Rōshi was requested to visit and they talked together on the level of spiritual experiences. Shinzan Rōshi recognised and acknowledged what Okazaki had experienced, but then pointed out that there was further to go. Gradually Okazaki began to open up. There was a foot in the door.

Over a series of prison visits Shinzan Rōshi helped him fully acknowledge what he'd done and begin to do what he could to make amends to the survivors. Okazaki became a Zen student. He is a gifted artist, and his ink paintings have appeared in the Gyokuryuji temple magazine.

Eventually the legal process progressed to the point that Okazaki's case was concluded. He was the first former *Aum Shinrikyo* cultist to receive the death sentence. At that point in the conviction process, Japanese law restricts prison visits to family members only. Undaunted, and believing that Okazaki could go further in his practice, Shinzan Rōshi adopted him as his son. Allowing such a hated person to become part of his family cost Shinzan Rōshi his marriage. Nevertheless, he stuck by his decision. At the time of writing Okazaki remains on death row awaiting execution. His Zen training continues.

Shinzan Rōshi has taught internationally for over 20 years. After naming me as a successor, he named a successor in Canada, Melody Eshin Cornell, and one in Japan, Tomio Yugaku Ameku. In May 2011 he came to London to witness the opening of Yugagyo Dojo, our Zendo Kyodan practice headquarters. In his speech of congratulations, he said:

'I believe that the Zen masters of the future could come from the students here. Nobody here is expecting money or fame; your motivation is sincere and your results will lead from that sincerity. May your practice and realisation bring you great happiness, and benefit all beings in the whole world.'

Shinzan Rōshi is a notable and collected Zen calligrapher. To honour his 80th birthday, his students in London organised an exhibition of his artworks. Contributors to the exhibition book[6] include Dr Audrey Seo, writer on Hakuin's art, and Professor John Stevens, perhaps the foremost Western commentator on Zen art and artists.

Over 80 years old, Shinzan Rōshi continues to reside as a hermit at Gyokuryuji. Although sometimes a little forgetful, his energy and vigour are undiminished. He runs every day, dotes on his dogs, and teaches all who come to him.

DAIZAN

When people ask me about how my connection with Zen began, I find myself tracing things back to an incident when I was seven years old. My family and I were on holiday in Cornwall on a beach called Cawsand. The beach is tiny, just room for perhaps five or six families on the sand.

In one of the families there that summer was a boy of 13 or so who was a very good swimmer. Every afternoon a passenger boat would come over from Plymouth bringing day-trippers. Every afternoon this boy would climb onto the boat as it was leaving, and just when it was out far enough that everyone would have a good view, he'd do a spectacular dive into the water.

---

6   Julian Daizan Skinner (2015) *The Zen Character: Life, Art and Teachings of Zen Master Shinzan Miyamae*. London: Zenways Press.

I thought of him as a terrible show-off and I was also pretty jealous because, despite loving the water, I couldn't quite swim.

I was in the sea one afternoon, up to my shoulders, and suddenly, out of nowhere, the tide turned. In a flash the water was over my head. I couldn't walk. Around my body a strong undertow or current was pulling me out to sea. But I could hold my footing. I needed to breathe. I jumped, broke the water surface, snatched a breath. I jumped again, this time really high. I caught some air, but there was no way I could do it again. It was obvious to me that I was about to die.

Something in me just gave up. I completely let go. At that moment, the universe just opened. I was loved, totally accepted, embraced in a vast acceptance that was bigger than life, bigger than death. It was utterly boundless. I knew I was completely safe.

And then, bang! An arm grabbed me. Before I knew it the show-off boy was dragging me in with a classic, perfectly executed life-save. As I sat on the beach, coughing (I'm not sure I even thanked him), I remember concluding, 'So that's where you go when you die, wonderful!', and then matter-of-factly carrying on with my holiday.

Being the sort of boy who got into scrapes, I found myself plunged into this boundless place once or twice again, but the thing was, none of it connected in my mind with religion, or spirituality. We were a church-on-Sundays Catholic family. But this seemed something different. So I just carried on with life. Nevertheless, a question got planted in me that day. Over the succeeding years, despite losing touch on a conscious level with what I'd found, this question quietly germinated. The substance of the question was: 'Can you live in that place or do you just have to wait until you die?'

All this was semi-conscious at best. Outwardly I was a relatively normal boy. I grew up in the part of England closest to France. It was the sixties and seventies – the height of the Cold War.

At this time the game of squash was becoming popular but there weren't many courts. My father was a keen player. His closest squash court was in the local Intelligence Corps army base. Most of his early squash games were against army officers.

I remember him coming home with stories of opponents mentioning that, any time the Russians chose to, they could roll across Europe and be in Calais within about 12 hours, and potentially across the channel in another day.

Our only option to stop them was the atom bomb.

This Cold War reality entered deeply into my consciousness. I didn't know how long we had; I just knew that there was a very real chance life would be short. I remember frequently waking up in the night convinced I'd heard the bomb go off and counting down the minutes until I realised it was just a heavy lorry driving by.

With this sense of the shortness and uncertainty of life, I wanted to experience as much as I could. I started by pursuing the conventional route. After graduation I worked as a scientist in the pharmaceutical business. It was a great job at a great company. I bought a house, met a beautiful woman, played the corporate game and, by my mid-twenties, felt I'd done it all. It wasn't that it was bad. In fact, life was good. My friends and family thought of me as a success. I just had a tremendous urgency to experience all of life as fast as possible.

Out of these two threads, the sense of boundlessness and urgency, came Zen. Through a dear friend, Rod Wooden, I discovered the beautiful open spaciousness of Soto Zen meditation. I found myself at home in the completely non-manipulative, utterly simple 'just-sitting' *shikantaza*[7] taught by Dogen Zenji, the Japanese Zen master who brought the tradition from China in the 13th century. It was just what my spirit had been calling out for.

Within a few months I'd sold my house, given away the money, said goodbye to my girlfriend and jumped into Zen monastery life. I trained at Throssel Hole, high up in the windswept expanse of the English North Pennine Hills. The teacher was Rev. Master Daishin Morgan.

The first seven years I lived with about 20 others in the *zendo*, the meditation hall. I had three feet by six feet of personal living space, a cupboard for bedding and a second cupboard for clothes. The monastery is a pressured environment. The image used to exemplify it was the rock tumbler – a kind of rotating drum filled with pebbles and stones that grind against each other, eventually producing beautifully polished jewels.

Apart from visits of a few months here and there to other Soto Zen establishments, I spent 14 years or so in the monastery.

Initially I had such a head of steam, I probably sat twice as much as anyone else. After a while my legs erupted in varicose veins. I had blood in my stool for a couple of years. But the urgency within wouldn't let me stop. In the sitting, my being unfurled into the silence, petal by petal.

Ten months after monastic ordination my view shifted and I directly saw that my previous sense of a fixed solid self was a laughable optical illusion. I perceived that everyone and everything was a dance of change. I was thrown into a purging of encrusted old views and feelings. It's hard to over-emphasise the physicality of this process. For several years it was apparent that only my youth was preventing

---

7   'Shikantaza', literally *shikan* – 'nothing but', *taza* – 'precisely sitting'.

my health from breaking down. At times the power running through me was so strong I barely slept. Over the years, I went up the monastic ranks. Eventually I received *dharma* transmission and permission to teach, and began the process of sharing what I'd found. I taught in the monastery, edited the magazine, and for periods of time ran branch temples and taught at associated *zazen* groups.

But as I began to teach, I realised one thing. For many people, this simple open sitting didn't work. I saw people a decade down the line of practice basically in the same place they started. Like putting a pot of cold water on a cold stove, nothing much happened. In the few cases where the stove was already lit, then the process unfolded beautifully. But otherwise, what people really needed was a means of ignition.

More than that, I noticed that in many instances the longer and more sincerely that people practised, the weaker and sicker they tended to become. I mentioned previously how at one point in a monastery where I was staying only one of the six monks forming the topmost tier was free of ME (myalgic encephalomyelitis), post-viral syndrome or other energy depletion conditions.

Added to this, the Soto Zen culture was very against discussing the enlightenment that was the outcome of practice. The emphasis was on the unity of practice and enlightenment in the moment – a true, but nevertheless one-sided, perspective.

I began looking into the methods of Rinzai Zen – traditionally a more dynamic approach focused on the spiritual opening called *kensho*, together with the ensuing deep and transformative work of embodying and expressing the understanding, all with a basis of mindfully managing the bodily energetics.

Seeking more 'cutting and polishing' for myself, I had the good fortune to meet Zen master Shinzan Miyamae, and went to practise with him at Gyokuryuji, the restored hermitage of the great 17th-century Zen master Bankei.

My decade-and-a-half of monastery experience counted for nothing. I went back down to the bottom of the pile in the small community of ten. Apart from Shinzan Rōshi himself, my fellow Zen students were mostly somewhat suspicious of the strange Englishman who had appeared among them, and despite the Japanese study I'd engaged in, I initially found a lot of what they said pretty incomprehensible.

I was assigned to work with the temple carpenter, Morimoto-san, a layman. Shinzan Rōshi had recently brought this illiterate, rough country workman to the experience of *kensho*. Morimoto was simply overflowing with love and kindness. When we were introduced, he looked deeply into my eyes, nodded his head and we laughed together.

From morning to night he was everywhere, helping people left and right. We could be up on the roof doing repairs, but somehow he would also have a job in the kitchen fixing the plumbing or he'd be bowing intensely in the Buddha Hall. It seemed like every time you went around a corner he was there, heart wide open, helping, helping, helping.

He took the awkward stranger under his wing, taught me how to use a Japanese-style saw, talked to me constantly in his country dialect, and beyond everything else he inspired me with the sheer wide open beauty of a life that is thrown into the universe, like a child throwing herself into her father's arms.

Gradually my grasp of Japanese improved as we discussed timbers and tools, weather and wind. We never spoke directly of spiritual experiences. Then one day, in his morning *dharma* talk, Shinzan Rōshi told the story of Eno, the great sixth ancestor of Zen. This man – a 7th-century illiterate mountain woodcutter – heard a monk chanting an important Buddhist text called the *Diamond Sutra* in the marketplace one day, and there and then realised *kensho*. 'These things still happen,' Shinzan Rōshi concluded, looking at Morimoto-san. 'Even right here. If you throw yourself into your practice, you will find it too.' The illiterate and uneducated Eno went on to become a brilliant and innovative teacher of *kensho*.

All this time, in *sanzen* (one-to-one interviews) with Shinzan Rōshi, I studied the *koans* of the Inzan line of Rinzai Zen. There were times when I felt unbelievably stuck – totally mired in impossibilities – and, usually completely unexpectedly, times when I was flying, passing *koan* after *koan* effortlessly. Rules didn't help here; instead Shinzan Rōshi constantly tried to draw forth in-the-moment resourcefulness. As soon as some kind of insight dawned, Shinzan he would urge (in English) 'Get and throw, get and throw' whilst acting out the motion of slinging any understanding over my shoulder. And the next *koan* would come. Any cognitive shift was discounted until it found embodiment and appropriate expression.

Temple life at Gyokuryuji was in stark contrast to my previous experience. Soto Zen encourages an adherence to forms, a certain punctiliousness, teaching that 'correct deportment is the Buddha *dharma*'. Shinzan Rōshi saw right through this and decided to un-stuff me. For months on end I never knew what was going to happen next. The only constant was the *koan*. Not only the *koans* Shinzan Rōshi gave me, but everyday life was a *koan* too, both in the temple and outside.

One autumn, Shinzan Rōshi sent me on pilgrimage. Shikoku is the smallest of the four main Japanese islands and intimately connected with Japan's greatest spiritual figure,

Kobo Daishi (774–835 CE). He introduced the Shingon school[8] to Japan and was hugely successful on many levels. He was born on Shikoku to an aristocratic family, but gave it all up to become a *hijiri*, a freelance holy man.

For centuries there was a dynamic in Japan where the *hijiri* would enter the mountains to meditate and pray, to recharge with the power of the mountains, the sky and the ancient forests – all personified as gods or Buddhas (or both), then returning to the walls and streets of the lowlands to bless the people in whatever way needed, sometimes even very practically by building wells and bridges. The pilgrimage is built around many of these ancient sites and focused the greatest *hijiri* of them all, Kobo Daishi.

His early training on Shikoku alternated between time in the temples studying and then meditating up in the mountains. Finally, at age 22, he succeeded in realising enlightenment in a sea cave. He was at Cape Muroto, which juts way out into the Pacific and is traditionally thought of as the place where dead spirits depart this world for the next.

He took the name Kukai, 'the Sky and the Sea'. Later he travelled to China and studied with a great Shingon master there, but his early life on the island is what caught the Japanese imagination, and for a thousand years *henro* or pilgrims have walked Shikoku. Over the centuries, the pilgrimage took form, and now the route has 88 temples connected by 1200 kilometres of travel.

The route is circular – in theory, endless. I decided to go the old-fashioned way, *nojuku* (sleeping outside), and living by *takuhatsu* (alms). I decided to only accept donations of food and not touch money during the pilgrimage.

---

8   The Japanese version of Vajrayana or Tantric Buddhism.

I was about a third of the way around the route when I made it to the cave where Kobo Daishi realised enlightenment. He could have moved out yesterday, it seemed so untouched. I spent a day and night there alone, meditating in the most exquisite peace I've ever experienced. My only company were the red crabs with huge expressive eyes (they're almost like cartoon characters), which abound down on the Cape.

Up to this point I had managed to keep up my self-imposed rule of not touching money at all. People kept wanting to put money in my alms bowl (Japan is really a cash economy) along with the peanuts and packets of crisps I ended up living on. In the end a man got so upset when I tried to refuse his money that he started crying. So I agreed and re-adjusted. I still planned to survive on alms, just to accept cash as well as food. It felt wonderful to at last be able to buy and eat some green vegetables.

On the walk I met farmers, monks and students seeking 'the true spirit of Japan', and many, many people newly retired and doing the route by bus. My most significant meeting was down on the huge peninsula of Ashizuri Misaki in the south west of the island.

To reach Temple 38, Kongofukuji, I'd struggled through a typhoon, an autumn storm, and was wet and tired. Nagasaki Shokyo, the temple master, noticed the soaked black-robed foreigner and took pity on me. After seeing to my survival needs he sat me down to talk. I explained how I'd been living on alms and my conflict about accepting money. He began to laugh. His laughing grew louder and louder. 'What's wrong with money?' he roared. 'You can't do much good wandering about wet and starving. Money is just another form of energy. You need to learn how to handle it. That's all.' Having given all my money away almost 20 years previously,

I was shocked. 'Learn about money.' He wasn't laughing now. 'Help many people.'

I walked on, still living out of my alms bowl, but a new perspective started to form. And it was still forming when, back at Gyokuryuji, on 5 November 2005, we had a massive fire. It started at noon, and within 45 minutes about half the temple was destroyed. We managed to save the main hall (just), but the connecting 400-year-old building containing the kitchen, office and accommodation for the senior people in the temple, as well as the temple tearoom, were reduced to ash and blackened timbers. We also lost one of the temple dogs, but all the humans made it through.

Probably the most critical time, from the human life point of view, was when Shinzan Rōshi rushed into the building and up the steep stairs to try to save his things. I knew that most fire deaths are caused by smoke and fumes. There was no way I was going to let him die on us, so I followed him in. His office was right near the source of the fire and already pretty smoky. 'Nani ga taisestsu?' I shouted at him. ('What's important?') He started grabbing things and putting them into my hands – his computer, robes, files, a small safe. I rushed each thing down the corridor to the far end of the building, but my thought was more on sticking with him – a 70-year-old man – and carrying him out if I had to. We got everything to the far end but the smoke was just overwhelming. 'Okay Rōshi,' I shouted. 'Ikimasho – abonai sugiru!' ('Let's get out of here, it's too dangerous!')

I bundled him down the stairs and out the door. He was okay, but within minutes everything we'd tried to save was engulfed in flames. Later, when we were working on the hoses to stop the flames engulfing the main Buddha Hall, he walked past me and said four words in English – 'Everything gone, but okay.' As he said this, he literally had just the robes on his back. All his papers, his formal robes, his computer, his passport – absolutely everything had been burned.

Like many Japanese people, he'd been fond of photographs. In the main office he'd had a shelf full of albums. The next day, sorting through the ash pile, I found them. The books were gone, but hundreds of singed and sodden pictures of his life were piled like autumn leaves.

The morning after the fire I came into the Buddha Hall at the normal time. The ceiling was badly scorched where flames had penetrated the roof space. Burning material had fallen onto the tatami matting on the floor, blackening it. A pall of old smoke still hung in the air. The main altar was covered in a blue tarpaulin. Shinzan Rōshi came in. No one else. We chanted together. After we'd finished we did *sanzen*, a one-to-one interview, right there, in the midst of the chaos. He said pointedly, 'I need a successor.'

It took some time to find the fire's cause. There was a young boy staying with us who had a growth defect. He was about ten years old, but looked (and thought) like half that age. The fire investigators discovered he'd been playing with matches in the garden, making little fires. One of them happened to be just too close to the building.

The next few months were filled with building jobs and recovery. I was amazed how Shinzan Rōshi himself didn't miss a beat. The rest of the *sangha* were badly affected. Initially we had no water, no telephone, no kitchen. November quickly turned into a hard, snowy winter. People were discouraged and cold. By January over half of the community was gone. It turned out that the number two in the temple, the person we'd all expected to take over, had forgotten to renew the building insurance. There wasn't a penny to cover the damage.

We were all terribly worried he'd kill himself. Fortunately he simply departed under a cloud.

I mentioned previously how, as we recovered from the fire, Shinzan Rōshi felt it was time to turn up the heat on me. He filled any empty spaces in the temple with homeless and mentally unstable people. I was *fuku jushoku* at the time – vice-abbot. Mostly he stood back and watched to see how I got on with bringing in the funds to keep these people fed and did my best to keep some sort of order in what was left of the temple. Life was particularly straitened by this time as the head temple, from which Shinzan had dissociated himself a few years previously, finally formally cut him off, which meant they could legally stop his pension and drain the temple bank account.

He cited previous self-sufficient exemplars, Zen master Ikkyu, who'd made money for his temple by painting the faces of dolls, Zen master Bukushu, who made straw sandals, and Zen master Sekiso, who became a potter. In my case I taught yoga and English in the local area, and this, together with *takuhatsu* (alms round), kept us all going. Time and resources were constantly stretched. I was surrounded by some extraordinarily eccentric people. I've never been so tested.

By the summer of 2007, my *koan* study was approaching the end. It had provided an education not only in realising the truth of things, but in expressing and embodying this truth. Not only had Shinzan Rōshi watched over my own understanding as it deepened, but he put a lot of energy into teaching me how to help others get their own understanding. He particularly taught me how to work with students in the delicate stage of being close but not quite there in their understanding. At the right moment it's possible to 'tip them over the edge'.

In a ceremony on 8 May, Shinzan Rōshi named and ratified me as his successor. In the first, private part of the ceremony he presented me with a certificate to that effect, and gave me the mission to find a successor in turn. 'People think becoming a Zen master is an end,' he said. 'It's a beginning. Start small. Don't try to do anything big. Just practise and open your door. Good people will come. Some people will just want a little – give them a little. Some people will want everything – I've seen that you can do that. The world is divided, split; your job is to find ways to bring people, nations to unity, to harmony.'

Then we joined with the other members of the community to make it public. There were many congratulations. But, truth be told, I was exhausted. I had a general sense that I could be most useful in the West, but beyond that, the way was obscure.

I left Japan mid-June. Remembering my pilgrimage on Shikoku, I decided to do something similar in the UK. On midsummer morning, 21 June, I set off, penniless, from St Catherine's Lighthouse at the south tip of the Isle of Wight and began walking northwards. My projected route was straight up the middle of the island of Britain, and the finish point was another lighthouse out on the high cliffs of Cape Wrath, northern Scotland.

I made it to Cape Wrath (old Norse for 'the turning point') a little over two months later. Imagine vast empty spaces – moorland and mountain reached across a rivermouth by motorboat. There's a tiny road winding 11 miles through the wind and rain and, at the tip, huge cliffs climbing a thousand feet out of the sea capped by a white lighthouse. As I crossed the water, the boatman said, 'With the tide and the wind, I'll be stopping in a couple of hours.' It looked like I wasn't going to make it back. I didn't have a sleeping bag or tent, or anything much to eat. 'Just find somewhere to sleep,' I thought.

So, after 11 miles and a pretty thorough soaking, I made it to the lighthouse. Finding a garage containing a rusted Toyota truck with the door ripped off (by the wind, I later discovered), I climbed in out of the wind and settled down for a nap. A few minutes later I was greeted by the barking of six springer spaniels and a Scottish voice telling them to shut up. That was my introduction to John the hermit, the occupant of the lighthouseman's accommodation, and the only human for hundreds of square miles. John graciously took in a soaked pilgrim, and we talked over macaroni cheese and toast by the light of a peat fire for a good bit of the night.

As the sun began to lower, the rain stopped and I was able to go out to the very tip of the Cape and chant the ancient scriptures of Zen. I took out a little stone that I'd carried from St Catherine's – the start point of the walk – and threw it far out into the sea.

When I sat in meditation, so many faces of the kind, generous, profound and extraordinary people I'd met over the previous 64 days appeared. Although I'd done the walking, their support made it possible, and just thinking of them I was moved almost to tears.

Then, in the wind at the end of the world, I danced.

Since then I've been in London. Zen students began to gather. Over this time, I've seen some wonderful developments – people finding the true basis of their lives and coming into flower. I've become increasingly convinced that Zen master Hakuin's framework of the two wings of a bird is uniquely suitable and practicable for people dealing with the stresses and strains of our Western culture.

As the West doesn't have a culture of support for serious spiritual practitioners like those you can find in Asian countries, I created a programme for students to become Zen yoga teachers and another for teachers of meditation. This way, students could earn a living within a context that would give them the time and scope to support their own practice, and make an offering that is of benefit to the world.

Our Zen meditation and mindfulness course has aroused interest in various quarters. The teacher training course gives new teachers the wherewithal to accurately pass on Zen meditation practices for health and wellbeing (traditionally known as *Bompu Zen*) as well as the material laid out in this book.

When people ask me to distinguish the two approaches, I often say that the health and wellbeing material is for problem-solving – whether we're talking about stress, insomnia, inability to relax, development of creativity, mental clarity and focus, whatever – all these fall under the heading of *Bompu Zen*. You can find more information at our website, www.zenways.org.

The other practices, the ones you have in this book, are for students who want to find the place where there never was a problem in the first place (you'll know by now that here, too, there's a strong emphasis on health and groundedness). Currently, our meditation material is the subject of a research project run by Dr Maryanne Martin and Dr Barbara Gabrys under the auspices of the Department of Applied Psychology at the University of Oxford. Preliminary results suggest that these practices are very good for you regardless of your level of engagement. I intend to write more about this in a companion volume on Zen practices for health and wellbeing.

Graduates of Zenways training have gone out and taught Zen meditation in the UK, Japan, the USA, the Netherlands and various other countries, at venues such as the Universities of Oxford and Westminster, the UK National Health

Service (NHS), charities including the former Kids Company and the St Giles Trust, companies such as BAE Systems and Support 2 Recovery, at colleges such as Imperial College, the Royal College of Art and the Royal College of Music, and many other locations.

Shinzan Rōshi often emphasised to me the importance of students developing a genuine understanding as quickly as possible. To this end, in his teaching he explored what he called 'group *sanzen*'. These days the term *sanzen* usually refers to teacher–student interviews, but literally means 'Zen study'. Shinzan Rōshi noticed that in the accounts of the old masters from the golden age of Zen in China, there was little mention of private interviews, but instead a range of free-flowing public interactions, sometimes between the master and a student in front of others, sometimes between the master and the whole group, and sometimes between students. Morning teaching sessions at Gyokuryuji became a forum for using these different permutations to investigate the way.

The last few years I have been building on Shinzan Rōshi's group *sanzen* experiments and combining them with American teacher Charles Berner's dyad process to create a 64-hour intensive Zen retreat format incorporating much of the work we've explored in this book.

The aim has been to present a process that is suitable for people from beginner level upwards that gives them a very real (over 50 per cent) chance of a direct awakening to the truth during the retreat. One of my Zen teachers once said to me when I presented an understanding to him, 'A little *daikon* is still a *daikon*.'[9] Even a small understanding can have a revolutionary impact. As I often say to my students here

---

9   A *daikon* is a Japanese radish.

in London, we could get on the train right now and have a day trip to Paris, and once you've been, even if it's as short as a day, you can never again be someone who's not been to Paris.

In addition, over the past few years I've been involved in the 'Managing Your Mind' programme of post-doctoral study at the University of Oxford, and more recently teaching health professionals at the College of Mindful Clinicians.

More than once Shinzan Rōshi has said to me, 'Practice in your seventies is so much deeper than in your sixties', emphasising that, even after half a century of practice, his road continues to unfold. I'm finding this too. I love the English legal term 'No visible means of support'. Step-by-step, moment-by-moment, the miracle arises. Shinzan Rōshi once said to me in his eccentric English, 'After all this hard training you become good man everybody like.'

TAKING THINGS FURTHER

If you find you'd like an audio visual course giving you more information and a more direct introduction to these practices, or if you'd like to become more connected with an active and vibrant community of Zen practitioners and even join Zenways as a student, or if you'd like to come on retreat with us, or come on a Zen trip to Japan, or if perhaps you'd like to train to teach the material we've been practising, or perhaps you'd like to purchase an original Zen artwork created by Zen master Shinzan – all these things and more can be found on our website at www.zenways.org.

GLOSSARY

Anapanasati (Pali): Mindfulness of the in-breath and out-breath. A fundamental Buddhist meditation practice believed to originate with the Buddha. It is claimed that it was this practice that led the Buddha to full enlightenment.

Bhikkhu (Pali): Monastic followers of the Buddha (female, *Bhikkuni*).

Dharma (Sanskrit): The truth, reality, and also used to denote the constituent elements of reality. Other shades of meaning feature in non-Buddhist uses of the term.

Do (Japanese): The way. Similar to the English, 'the way' can mean literally the road, and also has connotations of a way of life and the way of nature.

Dojo (Japanese): A practice hall or training ground.

Do-zen (Japanese): Moving Zen, Shinzan Rōshi's preferred term for Zen yoga.

Dukkha (Pali): A general longing for 'something more' from life; a desire to escape the grind and suffering of life. This could be seen as a sense of pervasive disappointment, and some have compared it to the existentialist idea of angst.[1]

---

1   See Brown, D., Loades, A. and Astley, J. (eds) (2003) *Evil (Problems in Theology)*. London and New York: T&T Clark Ltd, an imprint of Continuum.

Gotrabu nana (Pali): Change of lineage insight, the insight that projects the practitioner from the family of ordinary people to the family of noble ones – those who have entered the realm of enlightenment.

Hara (Japanese): Belly or guts, the physical and energetic centre of the human organism.

Hoshin koan (Japanese): A *koan* that is used to develop a direct connection with the *dharma* or reality of things, typically to provoke a first awakening or enlightenment.

Kanna-zen (Japanese): Meditation practice based on the contemplation of words, that is, a spiritual question or *koan*.

Ki (Japanese); **Qi** or **Chi** (Chinese): Energy, vitality.

Koan (Japanese): A spiritual question or problem, frequently non-logical or paradoxical, typically used as a theme for meditation or contemplation.

Missan Zen (Japanese): Literally 'secret study Zen'. The prevalent approach to studying Japanese Zen in the pre-modern era, strongly featuring private meetings between the master and student, in which esoteric matters of inner and outer cultivation were explored. It continues, to some degree, in certain lineages.

Mokusho-zen (Japanese): Literally, 'silent-radiance meditation', meditation practice that, in contrast to *kanna-zen*, is not based on the contemplation of a *koan*.

Naikan (Japanese): Literally, 'inner contemplation'. Hakuin's term for the energy cultivation practices he wrote about in *Yasenkana*.

Nanso no ho (Japanese): Soft ointment or soft cream meditation. A healing practice taught by the hermit Hakuyushi to the Zen monk Hakuin in the mountains outside Kyoto.

Nari-kiru (Japanese): Literally, 'become completely'. Frequently used in the context of *koan* study. When the student completely becomes the *koan* there is no longer any problem to be solved. When the gap between the student and reality is closed, there is an awakening to the non-dual nature of things.

Nen (Japanese): Mindfulness. Sometimes translated as 'attention', 'feeling' or 'sense'.

Nirvana (Sanskrit); **Nibbana** (Pali): The ending of suffering, the highest goal in Buddhism. Contemporary teacher Thannisaro Bhikkhu derives the term from the image of fire ceasing to cling to its fuel and becoming omnipresent.

Rikan (Japanese): Contemplation of reality. Hakuin's term for practices that open the gates of enlightenment.

Rinzai Zen (Japanese): The tradition of Zen originating with Chinese Master Rinzai in the 9th century. Emphasises the importance of clear-cut awakening and often strongly featuring *koan* study meditation practices.

Rōshi (Japanese): Literally, 'venerable teacher'. A term of address for a Zen master.

Samadhi (Sanskrit): Meditative absorption. A state beyond subject and object dualities. The term is used differently in non-Buddhist contexts.

Sange (Japanese): Recognition and conversion. The recognition of previous mistakes and the harmonisation of life with the highest truth (pronounced san-gay).

Sanzen (Japanese): Literally, 'Zen study', particularly referring to one-to-one interviews with the master.

Sesshin (Japanese): A retreat period devoted to intensive Zen meditation.

Shotaicho (Japanese): Literally, 'long nurturing of the sacred embryo'. A period of contemplative practice frequently in solitude, usually when *koan* study is substantially completed.

Soto Zen (Japanese): The Zen tradition originating in the 9th-century masters Tozan and Sozan; in modern times, strongly emphasising themeless open-minded *zazen* and the meticulous precision of everyday activities.

Susokukan (Japanese): Mindfulness of respiration through counting the breath.

Sutra (Sanskrit): Literally, 'thread a discourse', used in the title of many of the Buddha's teachings as well as others (related to the English word 'suture').

Taitoku (Japanese): Bodily attainment. A term for a matured and integrated condition of enlightenment.

Tanden (Japanese): Literally, 'elixir field'. A spot roughly three fingers' width below the navel in the centre of the body. The energetic and physical centre of the *hara*.

Tao (Chinese): The way. The Japanese equivalent is *Do*.

Yin/Yang (Chinese): Denoting the contrasting natures of elements within reality. For example, a hill is Yang in relation to a lake, but Yin in relation to a mountain. Yin and Yang, positive and negative, are never absolute states but always exist in relation to one another.

Zazen (Japanese): Literally, 'sitting meditation'.

Zendo (Japanese): A meditation hall.

Zenji (Japanese): Zen master. A term usually only used for the most senior (and often deceased) Zen masters.